THE ROYAL SHAKESPEARE COMPANY

The Royal Shakespeare Company is one best-known theatre ensembles.

The Company is widely regarded as one of the most important interpreters of Shakespeare and other dramatists. Today the RSC is at the leading edge of classical theatre, with an international reputation for artistic excellence, accessibility and high quality live performance.

Our mission at the Royal Shakespeare Company is to create outstanding theatre relevant to our times through the work of Shakespeare, other Renaissance dramatists, international and contemporary writers. Every year the Company plays to a million theatregoers at 2,000 performances, including over 50 weeks of UK and international touring.

We want to give as many people as possible, from all walks of life, a richer and fuller understanding and enjoyment of language and theatre. Through education and outreach programmes we continually strive to engage people with the experience of live performance.

The RSC's touchstone is the work of William Shakespeare. We are committed to presenting the widest range of Shakespeare's plays and demonstrating through performance the international and enduring appeal of his plays. We also want to inspire contemporary writers with the ambition of the Renaissance stage, presenting new plays alongside classical theatre.

The Company's roots in Stratford-upon-Avon stretch back to the nineteenth century. However, since the 1960s, the RSC's work in Stratford has been complemented by a regular presence in London. But Stratford and London are only part of the story. Over 25 years of residency in the city of Newcastle-upon-Tyne have forged a profound link between RSC artists and audiences in the north east of England. Many of our productions also visit major regional theatres around Britain. And our annual regional tour sets up its own travelling auditorium in community centres, sport halls and schools in towns throughout the UK without access to professional theatre.

While the UK is the home of the Company, our audiences are global. The Company regularly plays to enthusiastic theatregoers in other parts of Europe, across the United States, the Americas, Asia and Australasia. The RSC is proud of its relationships with partnering organisations in other countries, particularly in America.

Despite continual change, the RSC today is still at heart an ensemble Company. The continuation of this great tradition informs the work of all members of the Company. Directors, actors, dramatists and theatre practitioners all collaborate in the creation of the RSC's distinctive and unmistakable approach to theatre.

THE ROYAL SHAKESPEARE COMPANY

A PARTNERSHIP WITH THE RSC

The RSC is immensely grateful for the valuable support of its corporate sponsors and individual and charitable donors. Between them these groups provide up to £6m a year for the RSC and support a range of initiatives such as actor training, education workshops and access to our performances for all members of society.

The RSC is renowned throughout the world as one of the finest arts brands. A corporate partnership offers unique and creative opportunities, both nationally and internationally, and benefits from our long and distinguished record of maintaining and developing relationships. Reaching over one million theatregoers a year, our Corporate Partnership programme progresses from Corporate Membership to Business Partnership to Season Sponsor to Title Sponsor, and offers the following benefits: extensive crediting and association; prestigious corporate hospitality; marketing and promotional initiatives; corporate citizenship and business networking opportunities. Our commitment to education, new writing and access provides a diverse portfolio of projects which offer new and exciting ways to develop partnerships which are non-traditional and mutually beneficial.

As an individual you may wish to support the work of the RSC through membership of the RSC Patrons. For as little as £21 per month you can join a cast drawn from our audience and the worlds of theatre, film, politics and business. Alternatively, the gift of a legacy to the RSC would enable the company to maintain and increase new artistic and educational work with children and adults through the Acting and Education Funds.

For information about corporate partnership with the RSC, please contact Victoria Okotie, Head of Corporate Partnerships,
Barbican Theatre, London EC2Y 8BQ.
Tel: **020 7382 7132**.
e-mail: **victoria.okotie@rsc.org.uk**

For information about individual relationships with the RSC, please contact Graeme Williamson, Development Manager,
Royal Shakespeare Theatre, Waterside, Stratford-upon-Avon CV37 6BB.
Tel: **01789 412661**.
e-mail: **graemew@rsc.org.uk**

For information about RSC Patrons, please contact Julia Read, Individual Giving Manager,
Royal Shakespeare Theatre, Waterside, Stratford-upon-Avon CV37 6BB.
Tel: **01789 412661**.
e-mail: **julia.read@rsc.org.uk**

You can visit our web site at
www.rsc.org.uk/development

RSC EDUCATION

The objective of the RSC Education Department is to enable as many people as possible, from all walks of life, to have easy access to the great works of Shakespeare, the Renaissance and the theatre.

To do this, we are building a team which supports the productions that the Company presents onstage for the general public, special interest groups and for education establishments of all kinds.

We are also planning to develop our contribution as a significant learning resource in the fields of Shakespeare, the Renaissance, classical and modern theatre, theatre arts and the RSC. This resource is made available in many different ways, including workshops, teachers' programmes, summer courses, a menu of activities offered to group members of the audience, pre- and post-show events as part of the Events programme, open days, tours of the theatre, community activities and youth programmes. The RSC Collections, moved into a new home, will be used to create new programmes of learning and an expanded exhibition schedule.

We are developing the educational component of our new web site to be launched this year. The RSC will make use of appropriate new technologies to disseminate its work in many different ways to its many audiences.

We can also use our knowledge of theatre techniques to help in other aspects of learning: classroom teaching techniques for subjects other than drama or English, including management and personnel issues.

Not all of these programmes are available all the time, and not all of them are yet in place. However, if you are interested in pursuing any of these options, the telephone numbers and e-mail addresses are as follows:

For information on general education activities contact the Education Administrator, Sarah Keevill, on **01789 403462**, or e-mail her on **sarah.keevill @rsc.org.uk**.

To find out about backstage tours, please contact our Tour Manager, Anne Tippett on **01789 403405**, or e-mail her on **theatre.tours@rsc.org.uk**.

STAY IN TOUCH

For up-to-date news on the RSC, our productions and education work visit the RSC's official web site: **www.rsc.org.uk**. Information on RSC performances is also available on Teletext

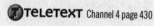 Channel 4 page 430

RSC MEMBERSHIP

Become an RSC Member and receive advance information and priority booking plus other exclusive benefits. Call our membership team on **01789 403440** for details of the various packages available, including UK membership, overseas, groups and education memberships. A free mailing list for those working in education is also available.

Night of the Soul was first performed by
the Royal Shakespeare Company in the Pit Theatre,
London, on 18 April 2002.
The original cast was as follows:

Nigel Betts	Terry
Tom Mannion	Francis Chappell
Hattie Morahan	Tracy
Cherry Morris	Doreen Chappell
Alison Newman	Liz Chappell
Will Tacey	Harold Chappell
Zoë Waites	Joanna
Alex Zorbas	Priest

Directed by	David Farr
Designed by	Angela Davies
Lighting designed by	Chris Davey
Music by	Keith Clouston
Movement Director	Liz Ranken
Sound designed by	Ian Dickinson
Music Director	Keith Clouston
Production Manager	Richard Howey
Costume Supervisor	Jane Dickerson
Company voice work by	Andrew Wade and Lyn Darnley

Company Stage Manager	Simon Dodson
Deputy Stage Manager	Martin King
Assistant Stage Manager	Marisa Ferguson

Musicians

Clarinet/wind synthesiser/ney	Larry Whelan
Percussion/ney/kaval	Tim Garside
Synthesiser/ud/Irish bouzouki/banjo	Keith Clouston

Night of the Soul

David Farr is a writer and director. As director he has focused on international work, and was Artistic Director of London's Gate Theatre from 1995 to 1998. Plays directed include *Seven Doors*, *The Great Highway*, *The Boat Plays*, *The Barbarous Comedies*, *Candide*, *Danton's Death* and *Leonce and Lena*.

As a writer, his play *Elton John's Glasses* premièred at Watford Palace Theatre in 1997 and won the Writers' Guild Best New Play of that season, opening in the West End in 1998. His play for children *The Nativity* premièred at the Young Vic Theatre at Christmas 1999. His play *The Danny Crowe Show* at the Bush Theatre, London, in 2001. His play *Crime and Punishment in Dalston* premièred at the Arcola Theatre in January 2002 in his own production.

DAVID FARR

Night of the Soul

faber and faber

First published in 2002
by Faber and Faber Limited
3 Queen Square London WC1N 3AU

Typeset by Country Setting, Kingsdown, Kent CT14 8ES
Printed in England by Mackays of Chatham plc, Chatham, Kent

A CIP record for this book
is available from the British Library

ISBN 0–571–21668–4

2 4 6 8 10 9 7 5 3 1

The sighs of death encircled me
The sorrows of hell surrounded me
In my tribulation I cried out

Psalms

Characters

2001

Joanna

Francis

Doreen
Francis's mother

Liz
Francis's sister

Terry

Tracy

A young couple

A lonely businessman

A weeping old woman

A gay man

A middle-aged woman in underwear

A beautiful young man

Commuters at Victoria Station

A widow

Mrs Wassermann
an elderly American tourist

Some drunken, flirty conferencees

Thomas
the ghost of Joanna's son

The final hotel guest

1983

Francis

Harry
Francis's father

Doreen
Francis's mother

1350

Joanna

Priest

Joanna's mother

Joanna's uncle

Friar

Villagers

*The play is written for a minimum of four actors
and four actresses*

*All names and events in this play are fictional
and any resemblance to real people, institutions
or places are coincidental*

NIGHT OF THE SOUL

Act One

ONE: BALLET OF THE HOTEL MERIDIAN

The year 2001. A large modern hotel in an English south coast town. The ground beneath the hotel: dark earth. Improvised wooden crosses, smashed and discarded. Bones. Skulls. Teeth.

A man and a woman enter a bedroom in the hotel. They kiss, and fall on the bed, rolling and grasping at each other.

A young woman appears dressed in modern hotel maid's uniform. She watches the couple but they do not appear to see her. She is Joanna. Joanna speaks to us.

Joanna I watch them. One and then another. They stay for a night, maybe a weekend. Then they're gone.

The couple roll off the bed, and are replaced by a lonely businessman on the telephone.

I hear their conversations.

Lonely Businessman Charlie, hi, yeah I've arrived, the meeting's not till tomorrow morning . . . I guess I'll just grab a burger downstairs . . .

Joanna I hear their thoughts.

Lonely Businessman (*still on phone*) I really want there to be a woman in the bar. Big tits, old enough to know the value of depravity. I want her to take me to her room, strip me and . . . (*Beat.*) Yeah, I think there's a Scottish match on Sky. Partick versus Morton.

The businessman rolls off the bed.

Joanna For some it's a refuge.

*An old woman enters the room, breaks down on the
bed and weeps.*

Joanna For others it's an opportunity.

*The old woman rolls off the bed, and is replaced by a
gay man preening himself in the mirror.*

For most it's just another hotel.

*He is replaced by a middle-aged woman in her
underwear smoking a cigarette, flicking through TV,
and drinking from a mini vodka bottle.*

Television The stegosaurus, with its scaly skin, and
aggressive temperament . . . (*She flicks the remote.*) Still no
sign of an end to this long and increasingly merciless . . .
(*She flicks.*) But I have a lemur to rescue! (*Huge canned
laughter, she flicks and rolls off.*)

Joanna (*beat*) But whoever they are, there's one thing
they have in common. They're all just passing through.

*A repeated cycle of the visitors, the lovers, the lonely
businessman, the crying woman, the gay man, the
middle-aged woman . . . faster and faster they enter
and leave the room . . . this is the repeated and endless
ballet of the hotel as witnessed by Joanna: our heroine.*

TWO: I WAS CLEANING THE TOILET

A beautiful young man enters and starts to undress.

Joanna The hotel opened in 1997. The town had
reinvented itself as a centre for information technology.
Investment was on the up, the beach had a blue flag and
the future was orange. Sixty-four rooms, mostly twin, but
with a few singles at the back where you get woken by
the kitchens at dawn. I watched them build it. I watched

the first guest arrive. A fifty-five-year-old systems analyst from a town called Coventry. He couldn't sleep because of an ulcer in his stomach, and I was divided between pity for his condition and the sheer joy of another human presence. Others followed. I'd never seen such money. Money was in their eyes. Their beautiful pale skin. Their glittering words. I learnt a whole new language. I practised it, repeating the words, the terms, getting the lingo. Several times I thought I fell in love. You can fall in love very quickly in a hotel.

The young man, now naked, enters the bathroom. He turns on the power shower. The power shower pours water on to the black earth.

The man enters the shower. Joanna approaches him and is almost touching him, his face, his hair, his body. The man is entirely oblivious to her presence.

The man disappears. Joanna stands, a bit wet, and dejected.

Well, it gets you down. To occupy myself, I started to clean the rooms. As soon as the guest checked out, I'd be there with my Jif and my Hoover. The chambermaids would walk in to find the room pristine. We've won sixteen awards for hygiene. I take a lot of satisfaction from that.

Pause.

Time is the cruellest torturer. When the hotel opened I thought it would save me. From my thoughts. From what I know. I walk the corridors day and night. But no one hears my step. No one catches my eye. I long to be mentally undressed. Once, in Room 23, I danced in front of a data processor as he was masturbating, just to feel it might be me he was thinking of. But it wasn't. Am I beautiful? I was. Am I horrific? I was. But now? Do I even exist? Can you see me? Can you?

5

Enter Francis Chappell, a forty-year-old man, with a small suitcase in one hand and a piece of paper in the other. Joanna is still in the bathroom. Francis puts down his suitcase, picks up the phone and dials.

Francis Estelle? It's me. I'm in the room.

Joanna Room 47. A businessman, hitting forty, married, here for the night, might bring a girl back, might not. Nothing strange. Nothing unusual.

Francis Listen. Will you listen? There's something I didn't tell you. She called me three weeks ago. She called my mobile. I was doing a pitch, I got her message on my voicemail. She said he must never know she called. She started to plead with me to come down and see him. She begged me. She's a proud bitch, my mother, but she was crying.

I don't know. I just don't know.

Can I call you later? You're going out? You got a baby-sitter? Great. Who are you going out with? With Jodie? Great. Did you kiss Thomas for me? I asked you to . . . it doesn't matter . . . it's fine. Yup.

He puts the phone down, checks his watch, takes off his trousers and shirt, turns to enter the bathroom. Joanna watches him unashamedly.

He sees Joanna. He cries out in surprise.

Francis Jesus Christ!

Joanna Aaah!

Francis What are you . . . What the fuck are you doing?

Francis has grabbed a towel. Pause.

Joanna Oh God. Oh God.

Francis What the fuck are you doing in my room? You must have heard me come in. You must have heard me on the phone. Were you listening?

Joanna shakes her head.

Were you listening to my conversation?

Joanna What are you doing?

Francis I'm calling the manager.

Joanna No! Please don't. I was just . . . cleaning . . . I was cleaning the toilet. (*to us*) My first words to another human being since . . . I was cleaning the toilet.

Francis And you don't do that before the guests arrive?

Joanna We do normally. I was late. I'm sorry. (*She lingers.*) Anything else, or do you think you could leave me alone?

Joanna You can hear me.

Francis Ears. Amazing things. You should try them.

Joanna You can see me.

Francis Goodbye.

Joanna Wait.

Francis No, I don't think so.

Joanna Please.

Francis Yes, thank you.

Francis ushers her out. Joanna exits slowly. Once out, she sits in shock.

Joanna He can see me. He can hear me. (*Beat.*) He can see me!

A joyous 'He can see me' dance along the corridor of the hotel. The room disappears.

Imagine. You're floating on an endless sea, your throat is burning, your legs scream with pain, but you can't die. Then, out of nowhere, comes an island, it's not much of an island, you've seen nicer islands, it could do with a palm tree or two, but for you at that moment, that small square mile of grey sand is paradise.

Wait! If he can see me, what about the others?

Tracy, a hotel receptionist at reception, stares blankly through Joanna.

All clear.

Joanna flicks through the computer.

Name. Francis Chappell. (*Beat.*) Francis Chappell. (*Beat.*) Address: Purley. Purley, where's Purley? We've never had someone from Purley. Here on business. Business. What business? It was all they had.

I had to go back.

Joanna steals the flowers at reception and returns upstairs. Immediately she is at the door of the room. She knocks. He opens.

Francis I didn't call.

Joanna I brought you these. Courtesy of the hotel.

Francis What for?

Joanna It's standard procedure.

Francis What is?

Joanna You know . . .

Francis It's standard procedure to spy on guests undressing and then give them flowers, is that what you're saying?

Francis's phone rings.

Hello? Estelle, hi. (*to Joanna*) Put them there. (*to phone*) What? Isobel just called? She was looking for me? Oh yes, I did call her, yes, about Jodie's number, well, I thought

8

you were going to Jodie's house, Estelle, calm down. It's not a big thing, wait . . . .

Francis enters the bathroom and shuts the door behind him.

Joanna I read a lot. It tends to be what I can find in the hotel – magazines and brochures. In brochures words are like mischievous children. They say what you want them to say but they don't really mean it. I began to think that maybe all words were like this now. And then I saw the piece of paper.

Joanna's eyes alight on the piece of paper.
She glances at it, then starts to read. Soon she is gripped. Then touched. Then deeply moved.

The language was like rich soil. It burst with meaning. Here was a man who felt what he described. And what he described was forgiveness.
Who was he?

THREE: I'M FRANCIS CHAPPELL

Francis Chappell, now dressed again, enters with a microphone and walks to the front of the stage. We are in a small viewing theatre in Coventry.

Francis Hi. I'm Francis Chappell. Thanks for coming. I know you've all got busy lives to lead so I'll try to make these two hours worthwhile. (*off mike*) That's how I always start. Nice and relaxed. Make them feel at home. Play a little game to warm them up. I've been doing this half my life, I know a few tricks. That day was no different. I played the game. (*on mike*) Separate into pairs. You don't need to move. Just find someone you've never met before. That's very important. Have we all found someone? Sir? Great. Now look at them and let

9

them look at you too. Don't be embarrassed. Nothing strange is going to happen. You won't have to kiss them. Look at their face, their clothes. Look in their eyes. Start to make some hunches about this person. Who are they? Where are they from? What do they do? How old are they? Are they with someone else here? Are they alone? Are they from a discernible social class? How do they vote? What religion are they? What sexual orientation? Do they smoke? Do they cook? Do they come here often? You're a detective, and you're searching for clues to the state of mind and body of this person.

Two minutes. And you've started to paint your picture. Now decide. What is it above anything else that this person wants? Could be a haircut. Could be a holiday. Could be great sex. A lasting and fulfilling relationship with someone who *really* understands them. A new mortgage? A new job? A new heart?

Make a decision. One thing you would give them if you could. Now tell them what it is. They won't reply. You will never know if you were right. Tell them now.

OK, you can relax.

What you've just done is a very simple piece of intuitive market research.

It is the dream of every company, every political party, every consumer group and polling organisation, to do what you've just done: to climb inside someone's head and find out what that person really wants.

Francis's beeper vibrates.

Sorry about this, I normally turn it off but I have some news coming from Leeds. (*He reads the message.*) And that isn't it. (*He laughs.*) Where was I? The dial. If you all look at the back of the seat in front of you, you'll see a dial. This is your love/loathe dial. I'm going to show you a film. I want you to react to every image you see. If you love it, turn it one way, if you hate it, turn it the other.

Francis's beeper vibrates again.

I'm really sorry. (*He reads the message.*) My wife. Again. (*He laughs. Beat.*) So: the love/loathe dial.

The beeper vibrates again. Francis looks at it again. It is clearly the same message.

Excuse me, I just have to sort this out. (*He calls on his mobile aware that the audience is listening in.*) Hi, it's me. Listen, I'm in the middle of a session, can I call you back? I know it's on, it's on in case Leeds call. (*Beat.*) Can't it wait? No, listen, I'll call you back. I said I'll call you back. (*Beat.*) What is so important? (*Pause. Francis listens, drops the mike, then suddenly sits down on the floor.*) OK. I think the best thing to do now. (*Beat. He takes the mike.*) What I normally like to do at this stage. (*Beat. Into the mike*) My father's dead.

FOUR: THE FUNERAL ORATION

A railway station. Francis is amidst a flurry of fast-moving commuters at Victoria railway station with a suitcase and talking on the extension to his phone.

Francis I decided to go . . . I know I said I wasn't going . . . I changed my mind! I'm at the station now . . . The funeral's tomorrow. I'll have to go straight to Birmingham after. Estelle, please let's not have an argument. Why? Because I don't want to look like one of those men at stations having an argument with his wife. I have a headache as it is. You're breaking up . . . I can't hear you. What did I say? I said I can't hear you. . . . It doesn't matter! I have to go. Kiss Thomas for me. Kiss Thomas for me!

Francis starts to run for his train. Others join him. The commuters each have a suitcase of their own now

*and there takes place a Commuter's Dance of Lament,
a fast but grieving dance, with Francis at its centre.*

    *Doreen Chappell is in her old armchair in a poky
living room in a first-floor flat of a crumbling
Victorian block along the seaside promenade of the
town. Doreen is sixty-seven, dressed in black, but with
a cheap red cardigan on top. A rug on the floor.
Another armchair stands empty.*

    Doreen is nervously smoking a cigarette.

Doreen What time is it?

Liz Five minutes later than when you asked me five
minutes ago.

    *Liz Chappell, daughter of Doreen, and Francis's sister,
thirty-nine years old.*

Doreen When's he coming?

Liz I told you.

Doreen I know. But when's he coming?

Liz He said he'd be here after seven.

Doreen What time is it now?

Liz Five past seven.

Doreen Maybe I'll go for a walk.

Liz Don't you want to be here when he comes?

Doreen Of course I do. But maybe I'll go for a walk.
After seven could be eight or nine.

Liz Or five past seven.

Doreen What will he look like? He'll be grey.

Liz He's only forty.

Doreen Why isn't he bringing his wife and child?

Liz You'll have to ask him.

Doreen But why? Doesn't the little boy want to meet his grandmother?

Liz It's been a long time. Maybe he wants to test the water.

Doreen He can have his old room.

Liz The sun's setting on the harbour. Come and have a look.

Doreen Harry junior can move in with you.

Liz I don't remember an evening as clear as this for years.

Doreen I'm not proud.

Liz Dad would have loved it.

Doreen Did you speak long? On the phone when he called. Did you speak long?

Liz We spoke.

Doreen But enough.

Liz Enough what?

Doreen Enough for him to get a measure of our status.

Liz Twenty minutes.

Doreen Of our standing in life.

Liz Maybe half an hour.

Doreen But enough for him to know things aren't easy.

Liz I think he knows that, Mum.

Doreen He can't expect luxury.

Liz We spoke mainly about the funeral arrangements.

Doreen We should have painted these walls. A lick of paint, that's what they need. Would have done it myself if you hadn't stopped me. New carpet. Good deals you can get on carpet down at Allied. Lick of paint and a bit of carpet.

Pause.

I don't want to see him. I don't want him here!

Liz It's all right.

Doreen I don't even know what he looks like. I don't know his face. Where is he? Where is he?

Francis is at the Hotel Meridian reception. He is greeted by Tracy, a young, uniformed, and relentlessly enthused female receptionist.

Tracy The television has a remote-control facility, the shower has hot water at all times of the day, and don't hesitate to call room service should you require assistance.

Francis (*to us*) There must be a course you go on to learn this kind of stuff: 'Pronouncing the Banal. In six weeks you will learn how to meet and greet consumers in a variety of modern leisure locations.'

Tracy On behalf of Meridian Hotels, it's a pleasure to serve you.

Francis (*to us*) How many times had I heard it? The same singalong voice, the same glazed eyes. It felt like any night in any hotel in any English town. It just happened to be my own.

Tracy Here on business, are you?

Pause.

Francis Yes, that's right.

Tracy What's your line of work, if I may ask?

Francis I work for a market research agency.

Tracy Oh right. That must be interesting. Is it interesting?

Francis I don't remember this hotel.

Tracy It's pretty new in actual fact. It was built five years ago as part of the Regeneration of Local Heritage programme. It's a terrific programme, a partnership between local businesses and the council to promote the profile of the town through initiative and enterprise, perhaps you've heard about it?

Francis No I haven't.

Tracy My friend's dad is the deputy marketing manager. He has a lot of burgeoning ideas. You should meet him.

Francis I'd be glad to.

Tracy That's how I got the job. I want to be in the tourist industry. Did you know that tourism is responsible for six per cent of national income, more than cars and shipbuilding combined?

Francis No, I didn't.

Tracy That's why hospitality and customer care are so important. A country can be judged on how it treats its visitors. Who said that?

Francis I think you did.

Tracy Yes, I know, but before me. Someone must have said it.

Francis Listen. Can I leave this with you?

Francis leaves his suitcase with Tracy. In Doreen's room, the buzzer goes.

Doreen You go.

Liz goes out. Doreen straightens herself. A clearly very moved Liz enters, and behind her Francis. Mother stares at son. Son stares at mother.

Francis.

Francis (*to us*) Try as you might, you can't picture your mother a second older than when you last saw her.

He looks at her. She looks at him, then turns away. He looks at the room.

Francis (*to us*) They'd not decorated since I left. The same smell of boiled celery. The same curtains, greyer, mustier. The china dogs in the glass cabinets were sparkling.

Pause.

The same chair. The same rug. The same.

Doreen Travelling light, are you?

Francis No, I left everything at the hotel.

Pause.

The hotel.

Francis I thought since Harry junior has my room . . .

Doreen Harry junior can move in with his mother.

Francis It seemed easier. Liz has the wake to prepare . . . I would only get in the way.

Doreen You and Harry junior can share the same bed for one night, can't you, Liz?

Liz Mum. If he wants to stay in a hotel, he can.

Doreen Of course he can. He's a free man in a free society, he's free to do what he wants. Which one's he staying in?

Francis I'm staying in the new one on the ring road. The Meridian.

Doreen Dear, that is. He doesn't want to go there.

Liz I'm sure he can afford it.

Doreen Oh he can, can he?

Liz You look good.

Francis So do you. Both of you.

Doreen Never felt better.

Liz Mum.

Doreen So . . . you'll be staying for the funeral and then . . .

Francis I have to leave tomorrow. I have a focus group in Birmingham.

Doreen He's a busy man.

Liz Do a lot of travelling, do you?

Francis A fair bit.

Doreen (*beat*) I thought after the wake we'd go out on the boat. Take you out to the lighthouse. See the beginning of the ocean.

Francis Can you still do that?

Doreen I can.

Liz You want tea, Francis?

Francis You can call me Frank.

Liz I'll make tea.

Doreen You haven't met Harry junior, have you?

Francis Liz was telling me about him.

Doreen He's a good lad.

Liz Describe the ways in which he is a good lad.

Francis What's he doing with himself?

Doreen It's a humiliation. When my Harold was young, a man didn't do that kind of work. That was left to the immigrants.

Pause.

Francis Can I do anything? For the . . .?

Liz No, it's all arranged, thanks.

Doreen Liz has been a marvel, she has.

Francis (*re Liz being a marvel*) So what's new?

Doreen (*out of nowhere*) We knew he was going. Best thing for him, he hated being looked after. Never could stand people fussing. Didn't want a funeral at all. 'Dump me in the sea, and let the fish have me.' That's what he said.

Pause.

Be a good crowd tomorrow. People remember Harry Chappell. How many you say are coming, Lizzie?

Liz Over a hundred, I reckon.

Doreen A hundred. We had a man walk up to us in the street, and say, 'Mrs Chappell,' he said, 'you don't know me but I used to work with your Harry in the sixties. In the docks before they brought in the containers.' He said, 'I'd be very grateful if you would allow me to pay my respects on Wednesday morning.' Thirty years he hasn't seen Harry. And still he wants to pay his respects. That's decency for you.

Pause.

Francis Did you . . .?

Doreen What?

Francis I sent . . . a couple of times . . . I sent you a letter. But you never . . .

Doreen No. We never cashed it.

Pause.

Francis (*to Doreen*) Well I should probably . . .

Liz What, already? I mean. If you want.

Francis I have some work to finish . . . and I'm sure you have stuff to . . .

Doreen (*getting up*) Sit down, Frank.

Francis does not sit down. Doreen goes into her bag, takes out a folded piece of paper, hands it to him. Liz looks on in surprise.

Francis What's this?

Liz What is it, Mum?

Doreen It's the funeral oration.

Liz The what?

Doreen I wrote it myself. I don't know about the spelling.

Liz When did you write it?

Doreen I've been thinking about it for a while. Why don't you read it?

Francis You're speaking at the funeral?

Doreen No, Frank. You are.

Francis reads the piece of paper. His face is filled with horror.

FIVE: DOGS AND FLOWERS

Francis is speaking on the phone in the street. He has the speech in his hand. There is light rain.

Francis But what do I do, Estelle? (*to us*) My wife. I always call her in a crisis, it's a reflex, and like all reflexes, after a while, you begin to wonder why it's there. (*to Estelle*) She's written this reconciliation scene. According to her I came up to see him the day before he died. According to her I spent the whole day at his bedside and everything came out – the argument, what he said, what he did. Apparently he asked me to forgive him. Apparently I did. Apparently we shook on it, he hugged me, I hugged him and it was all just peachy. Then, listen to this: 'This done, my father whispered that having made his peace with his son, he could make his peace with God. And taking my mother's hand in his, he closed his eyes and died.'

But what do I do? It transpires that she's been telling all her friends to expect a surprise at the funeral. She's been doing a fucking spin campaign on the fucking speech. 'My son will say how moved he was, my son will go on to say how relieved he is that all this has finally been sorted out.' Yes, of course I wish it had been sorted out. I know I was always saying I should go. But I never went!

Pause.

I'm sorry. I shouldn't be shouting at you.

You know what the worst part is. It's beautiful. My mother is a wonderful writer.

A jogger is staring at Francis. Francis stares back.

Listen. The battery is going. I'll call you back.

Francis hangs up. The man is also forty, but large and unfit.

Terry Frank? It is Frank, isn't it? Frank Chappell?

Francis Yes. (*to us*) Who is he? Who the fuck is he?

Terry Terry. Terry Marshall. Terry?

Francis Terry! (*to us*) No idea. (*to Terry*) How are you, mate?

Terry Yeah yeah, not bad, yeah. You?

Francis Good, yeah.

Terry That's good.

Francis Yeah.

   Pause.

Terry Haven't seen you around . . .

Francis I haven't lived here for a while.

Terry Well, that would explain it then.

Francis (*pause*) How about you?

Terry Oh yeah. I'm still here. Yeah. Went to Bournemouth for a while.

Francis Did you?

Terry Yeah. Came back though. (*Pause.*) Well . . .

Francis Well . . .

Terry See much of Biggsy?

Francis No.

Terry No, nor me. He was a right cunt, wasn't he? Good old Biggsy.

Francis (*to us*) Now I knew. Terry Marshall. Cock like a Greek pillar. Terry Marshall. (*to Terry*) Jogging, are you?

Terry Just started. Thinking of doing the marathon.

Francis Good luck.

Terry Well, it's an aim. Look here. This tells me my heart rate.

Francis Great.

Terry It doesn't work in the rain.

Francis Listen, Terry, I should really . . .

Terry Yeah, listen, I should really . . .

Francis Right.

Terry Yeah.

Francis Good to see you though.

Terry D'you hear about Colin McGeechan?

Pause.

Francis (*to us*) Why bring him up?

Terry You didn't hear about that?

Francis No, what?

Terry I thought you would have heard.

Francis Heard what?

Terry Threw himself off a bridge.

Francis He . . . what? (*to us*) Relax the face. Breathe. Everything will be fine.

Terry That's what they say. Listen, where are you staying?

Francis Me? I'm . . . I'm at the Paramour. The old hotel on the main strand.

Terry That's closed, mate.

Francis Not the Paramour. The one just along from it.

Terry The Phoenix.

Francis Yeah.

Terry Don't envy you. I fixed the pipes in there once. Right old mess they were. Well . . .

Francis (*to us*) Don't ask about McGeechan. Don't ask. (*Pause. To Terry*) About McGeechan . . .?

Terry Don't know much. Read it in the paper. They brought up that thing with your dad's dog again. Course it was never proved. And never proved. But he was always a bit weird. Been on the pills for a good while, so they say. What you doing tonight? I might pop round.

Francis Well the thing is . . .

Terry Have a drink in the bar. Relive a few memories.

Francis I won't be back until at least eleven.

Terry I'll pop in around eleven, then. The Phoenix!

He jogs off. Francis is standing silently.

Francis Put it out of your mind. You've got enough on your plate.

Tracy Hotel Meridian, how can I be of service?

In the Hotel Meridian, Francis has picked up his suitcase from reception, enters his room, puts his suitcase down, goes to the phone and dials.

Francis Estelle? It's me. I'm in my room.
  Listen. Will you listen! There's something I didn't tell you. She called me three weeks ago. She called my mobile. I was doing a pitch, I got her message on my voicemail. She said he must never know she called. She started to plead with me to come down and see him. She begged me. She's a proud bitch my mother, but she was crying.
  I don't know. I just don't know.

Can I call you later? You're going out? You got a baby-sitter? Great. Who are you going out with? With Jodie? Great. Did you kiss Thomas from me? I asked you to . . . it doesn't matter . . . it's fine. Yup. (*He puts the phone down.*) I needed a shower.

He takes off his trousers and shirt, and turns to enter the bathroom. Joanna watches him unashamedly.
He sees Joanna. He cries out in surprise.

Francis Jesus Christ!

Joanna Aaah!

Francis What are you . . . What the fuck are you doing?

Francis has grabbed a towel. Pause.

Joanna Oh God. Oh God.

Francis What the fuck are you doing in my room? You must have heard me come in. You must have heard me on the phone. Were you listening?

Joanna shakes her head.

Were you listening to my conversation?

Joanna What are you doing?

Francis I'm calling the manager.

Joanna No! Please don't. I was just . . . cleaning . . . I was cleaning the toilet.

Francis And you don't do that before the guests arrive?

Joanna We do normally. I was late. I'm sorry.

She lingers.

Francis Anything else, or do you think you could leave me alone?

Joanna You can hear me.

Francis Ears. Amazing things. You should try them.

Joanna You can see me.

Francis Goodbye.

Joanna Wait.

Francis No, I don't think so.

Joanna Please.

Francis Yes, thank you.

> *Francis ushers her out. Joanna leaves. Francis goes to his bag, takes out aspirin, swallows two.*

(*to us*) Estelle and I have been married for twelve years. I spend a lot of nights away. It's part of my work, making pitches, doing focus groups. That's when she sees him. It's been going on for just over six months. She doesn't know I know. Normally I wouldn't even bother to check. But this wasn't work. This was my father's funeral. Surely she wouldn't . . .? (*Beat.*) I didn't have Jodie's number. (*Francis dials.*) Hi, is that Isobel? Isobel, hi, it's Francis. Yeah, how are you? Listen, Estelle's gone over to Jodie's, she's left her mobile here at home, and I need to talk to her. Do you have Jodie's number? Thanks. Great. Two-four-seven. OK. Yes we must. Absolutely. 'Bye now.

> *He has written the number down on a piece of hotel paper. He picks up the phone to dial but there is a knock at the door. He opens the door. It is Joanna with a large bunch of flowers.*

I didn't call.

Joanna I brought you these. Courtesy of the hotel.

Francis What for?

Joanna To apologise. It's standard procedure.

Francis What is?

Joanna You know.

Francis It's standard procedure to spy on guests undressing and then give them flowers, is that what you're saying?

Francis's phone rings.

Hello? Estelle, hi. (*to Joanna*) Put them there. (*to phone*) What? Isobel just called? She was looking for me? Oh yes, I did call her, yes, about Jodie's number, well, I thought you were going to Jodie's house and I wanted to talk to you. Estelle calm down, it's not a big thing . . . wait . . . (*Francis enters the bathroom and shuts the door behind him.*) You'll have your mobile on you? Of course you will. I know you always have it. I'm just tired. Why did Isobel call? She told me the wrong number? Oh did she? Oh I see. Well, have a good night. Give the sleeping angel a kiss from me. Love you too. (*to us*) My first mistake. Did she suspect?

Francis returns out of the bathroom and sees Joanna reading the speech. She doesn't see him. Pause.

Francis What the hell are you doing?

Joanna Sorry. I'm sorry.

Francis I don't believe this.

Joanna I'm really sorry.

Francis Give me one reason why I shouldn't report you.

Joanna I didn't really read it. I was just skimming.

Francis What is wrong with you?

Joanna It's complicated.

Francis I don't want to know. Just get out of my room.

Joanna (*beat*) It's beautiful.

Francis What?

Joanna What you've written. That you can love someone so much to overcome that anger, to hold them in your arms . . . to forgive them . . .

Francis . . .

Joanna No please, don't say anything. I'm sorry. I should never have read it.

Francis I don't believe this is happening.

Joanna I should go. I'm going.

Francis Now you listen to me. You walk out this door, and you say nothing to anybody about what you've just read. Is that clear?

Joanna I understand.

Francis What do you understand?

Joanna You want it to be a surprise.

Francis Just go away.

   Pause.

Joanna No.

Francis Excuse me?

Joanna I'm sorry. It's been so long.

Francis Why are you crying?

Joanna I don't know. It seems too strange.

Francis Listen, I'm sure you have genuine problems . . .

Joanna You forgave him? You really forgave him?

Francis Listen . . .

Joanna Joanna.

Francis Joanna. I am trying not to lose my patience.

Joanna We were destined to meet.

Francis Only in the sense that you hid in my bathroom.

Joanna What are you doing tonight?

Francis My father's being buried tomorrow, I thought I'd have a wild party in my hotel room.

Joanna Have a drink with me.

Francis Have I not made myself clear? I want to be alone!

Pause.

Joanna Greta Garbo.

Francis What did you say?

Joanna Nothing.

She leaves. Francis sits on the bed and thinks.

Francis (*to us*) Don't call Isobel again. It's better not to call.

He takes out the black suit for the funeral, and hangs it up. He looks at it. He turns on the television.

Television What card is accepted in more than four thousand countries . . . (*He flicks.*) Still no sign to an end in this long and increasingly merciless . . . (*He flicks.*)

Francis turns off the television and picks up his phone. Dials.

Francis Isobel? It's Francis. Hi. Yeah, sorry, there was a confusion, did I say I was at home? I was still at work. Listen, just to confirm the right number for Jodie. Thanks. OK. Thanks.

Francis dials the number.

Jodie, is that you? Hi, it's Francis. Listen, what are you doing tonight? . . . Nothing. You're sure? No, I just wondered. We'll speak soon. OK. 'Bye.

Francis sits deep in thought. The black suit hangs above his head.

It was hardly the first time. But this time, it hit me like a black hole. My wife having an affair, and not trying hard enough to hide it. Did she want me to find out? Did she want out? And Thomas?

SIX: THE BLACK DEATH

Joanna is in the foyer.

Joanna (*to herself*) Too quick! Too sudden and up front! Greta Garbo! Idiot! Get a grip on yourself or you'll lose him for ever!
(*to us*) Only once before had something like this happened. A woman had come to the hotel not long after it opened.

A middle-aged woman in dark glasses has arrived at reception and Tracy is talking to her.

Tracy A country can be judged by the happiness of its children. Who said that?

Woman I don't know.

Joanna I was listening, in the foyer. She turned and looked at me. At once I knew she was a widow.

The woman approaches Joanna in amazement.

Tracy I need your signature. Excuse me, I need your signature.

Woman What?

Tracy I need your signature.

Woman Yes, of course.

Joanna And, as if by magic, I was gone. I hadn't moved, but I knew she couldn't see me any more. Tracy had seen to that. I had lost her.
I will not lose him.

In the hotel room Francis is dialling the phone.

Francis Is that reception? I just spoke to one of your maids, and she left something in my room, could you send her up here please? Her name's Joanna. What do you mean, you have no one of that name working here? I just spoke to her. Do you not know who works in your own hotel?

He puts down the phone. Joanna knocks at the door.

Francis Who is it?

Joanna Listen, it's me again, I have to talk to you, please let me in.

Francis goes to the mirror, checks his appearance, rushes to add aftershave, sprays, checks again. He opens up casually.

Francis Come in.

Joanna You must think I'm stalking you. I'm not.

Francis They don't know who you are at reception.

Joanna What do you mean?

Francis I asked. They said there was no Joanna working here.

Joanna They must have forgotten me. It's quite a big staff.

Francis (*to us*) Why had I called? Why this sudden fear of being alone? Normally there's nothing I like more than my own company.

(*to Joanna*) Are you still on duty?

Joanna No.

Francis Would you like to have that drink with me?

Joanna I thought you hated me.

Francis More of a mild dislike. Shall we go?

Joanna You mean downstairs?

Francis Is there a problem?

Joanna It's just I work here. The bar isn't that special for me.

Francis Well, we'll go somewhere else. Get something to eat.

Joanna No, I can't. (*Beat.*) I'm working later. I shouldn't go too far. Can't we have it in here?

Francis You want to have a drink in here?

Joanna Yes.

Francis A complete stranger, in his hotel room . . .

Joanna Yes, I know.

Francis The challenge is normally to get a girl *into* one's room.

Joanna You have to take me as you find me. Is that the right phrase?

Francis Are all the chambermaids like you?

Joanna No.

Francis That's probably just as well. What would you like?

Joanna Whatever you're having.

Francis pours the drinks.
He hands her a drink and touches her hand. She recoils, sits down.

Francis (*to us*) Too quick. You're out of control, man. (*to her*) Are you all right?

Joanna Yes!

Francis I don't normally do this. I mean I don't want you to think . . .

Joanna I don't mind.

Francis I just feel like some company. I don't want you to think . . .

Joanna I don't think anything.

Francis But when I touched you . . .

Joanna Touch me again.

Francis moves towards her, does so.

Francis Is that OK?

Joanna (*beat*) You can explore elsewhere if you want.

He does so. They move to kiss. But suddenly she pushes him away and recoils in shame.

Francis What is it?

Joanna Nothing. Sorry.

Francis What's wrong?

Joanna I just suddenly thought . . .

Pause.

I didn't want you to catch . . .

Francis Catch what?

Joanna Nothing.

Francis Catch what?

Joanna Nothing.

Francis Catch what?

Joanna turns to us.

Joanna Before the hotel was opened, the site had been derelict for fifteen years. Before that it was a paper mill, dating from the Industrial Revolution. Before that wasteland, before that marsh, and before that . . .

Men and women of the fourteenth century crawl out from the hotel's woodwork.

The news first came from a travelling friar who had heard from a man in Normandy that thousands were dying in a place called Italy. The disease had come on a boat from the East, no one knew how it spread, but it seemed to be consuming the world. The stories told of mountains of bodies, cemeteries brimming over, dogs and babies lying dead on the streets. We didn't believe it. There were always horror stories. And anyway, Italy, such a long way away, it meant nothing. Then, one night, a rider galloped into town.

A man on a dark stallion rides through the coastal mists.

He'd come from along the coast. He said two words.

Rider It's here.

Music of Requiem. The people prostrate themselves in prayer. The parson speaks the sermon.

Parson There has come to this land a plague sent from God to punish us for our wickedness and our greed.

Look to your souls and witness there the seeds of the plague. Witness there the sin that opens wide its arms to the mists of death.

Joanna Two days later the town baker collapsed in his shop.

One of the peasants falls choking and coughing on the minibar. Others rush to him and place him on the bed near Francis, who sees none of this.

When they examined him, they found red lumps growing under his arms and in his groin. The next day he started to spit blood. His arms shook uncontrollably and a fever raged in his head. The day after, the growths burst and the poison poured out on to the floor. Then his lungs gave in. In three days he was dead.

The body is covered.

Within two months the cemetery was full. The parson had fled. A visiting friar agreed to consecrate a piece of land outside the town. Bodies were buried with speed, dumped into a large trench left open for the purpose. Men, women and children piled up in a mass grave and left to the worms.

The peasants pile themselves up on the hotel bed in a mass grave.

Here. Where I stand. Bones and teeth. People I know. People I loved. Thomas . . .

SEVEN: WHAT DO YOU WANT?

The bodies are still there but Francis does not see them.

Francis Catch what?

Joanna A cold. I have a cold.

Francis Is that all?

Joanna It's quite a bad one.

Francis I have some aspirin.

Joanna I'm fine.

Francis This must be illegal, mustn't it, drinking in a guest's room?

Joanna Yes. I expect it is.

Francis Well, I promise not to tell.

Joanna When's the funeral?

Francis Tomorrow. Why?

Joanna And then what, you leave?

Francis Straight after.

Joanna So tonight is all we have.

Pause. He moves closer to her.

Francis I find you very attractive, Joanna.

Joanna Really?

Francis Yes.

Joanna You don't know how much that means to me.

They kiss, then kiss passionately, then she pulls away.

Francis Are you all right?

Joanna Did you love him?

Francis Who?

Joanna Your father. I mean whatever happened, to have forgiven like that, you must have loved him deeply.

Francis I'd rather not talk about it.

Joanna What did he do to you?

Francis I said I'd rather not talk about it.

Joanna Sorry.

Francis Listen. Why don't you relax?

Joanna Francis . . .

Francis You know my name?

Joanna I read it on the computer. Francis, do you think that however serious a crime a person has committed, they can be forgiven?

Pause.

Francis Excuse me?

Joanna I mean: can a sin be so bad as to be unforgivable?

Francis Is this always how you chat up men?

Joanna I don't chat up men.

Francis I don't believe in sin.

Joanna What do you believe in?

Francis I don't know.

Joanna You must believe in something.

Francis I suppose I believe in freedom.

Joanna Freedom?

Francis That we all have a right to pursue what we want so long as it doesn't damage others.

Joanna But you wrote that you forgave your father. Look, you wrote . . .

Francis I know what I wrote.

Joanna He must have done something wrong to merit the need for forgiveness.

Francis We argued, he said something he shouldn't have said . . . he did something he shouldn't have done.

Joanna What did he do?

Francis Listen. I didn't I ask you in here to talk about my father. (*to us*) She didn't answer. But I felt a door open, as if we were starting down a road I had never intended to travel, and from which I could never return. (*to her*) Have you done something wrong?

Joanna nods.

Do you want to tell me about it?

Joanna shakes her head.

Why were you in there? Why are you always coming back here?

Joanna You won't understand.

Francis I spend half my life trying to understand people. It's what I do.

Joanna Understand what?

Francis What they want from life. What will make them happy.

Joanna Do you think you can understand what I want?

Francis What do you mean?

Joanna Try to find out.

Francis You could just tell me.

She smiles. Francis, to us:

The challenge excited me. She seemed to be always disappearing. A road stretching into the distance, endlessly receding. (*to her*) All right. Think of the one thing you really want. In two minutes I'll know what it is. Do you have it?

Joanna Oh yes.

Francis OK. How old are you?

Joanna Twenty-three.

Francis Where were you born?

Joanna Just down the road.

Francis And you've lived here all your life?

Joanna Yes.

Francis Never felt the urge to spread your wings?

Joanna It's not an option.

Francis You don't get paid enough. Do you live with your family?

Joanna I live alone.

Francis No boyfriend? Do you want one?

Joanna I'd like to be close to someone.

Francis You're lonely? It's OK to say.

Joanna Yes.

Francis Do you like the way you look? I mean the way you look, do you like it?

Joanna I don't know. I can't see myself.

Francis You mean you judge yourself by how others see you.

Joanna No, I just can't see myself.

Francis Do you drink a lot?

Joanna No.

Francis Take drugs?

Joanna I really don't need to.

Francis Do you like sex? If you don't mind . . .

Joanna No. And yes.

Francis What about hobbies?

Joanna Movies.

Francis You mean films.

Joanna Films, yes. I watch them whenever I can.

Francis Old ones, new ones?

Joanna They're all new to me.

Francis What else?

Joanna Sometimes late at night, I go on the Internet.

Francis You're on the net?

Joanna The hotel is. There's a music web-site. Modern music. I love jungle.

Francis You love jungle.

Joanna Oh yes. At five o'clock the night porter sneaks off for a cigarette outside. I have about five minutes. I play a track. And I dance in the foyer.

Francis You dance to jungle music in the foyer?

Joanna Yes.

Francis And no one's caught you?

Joanna No.

Francis Couldn't you dance at home?

Joanna This is my home.

Francis You see the hotel as your home?

Joanna It is my home.

Francis What do you fear most?

Joanna Hell.

Francis You believe in God?

Joanna Yes.

Francis No one believes in God.

Joanna They should.

   Pause.

Francis Time's up.

Joanna Well? What do I want?

Francis I think I know. (*to us*) I thought I did. When you've done this a lot, you can get a hold of a person pretty quickly. I have a system. I call it the animal kingdom. At the top of the tree are the proud panthers, ruthless, out for the kill. Then there are the graceful gazelles, my wife's a gazelle, nothing gets to her, it's as if she's always somewhere else. Further on down are the cockatoos, they're the party girls, the guys in Hawaiian shirts. Then there are the worker bees. That's me. Never resting. Never still. And then there are the caged birds. That was her.

Joanna A caged bird?

Francis Don't you want to be free?

Joanna Yes.

Francis But what will give you freedom?

Joanna Go on.

Francis You want to be an actress. Am I right? You want to get to drama school but you're too scared or poor or both to apply. Am I right?

40

Joanna Good try.

Francis It's some kind of performance. Dance!

Joanna No.

Francis Music. You want to sing. You want to be in a girl band!

Joanna Not quite.

Francis What then? What?

Pause.

Joanna I want to die.

EIGHT: I LOVE THE MOVIES

Joanna turns to us.

Joanna It's true. I love the movies.

The bodies flee from the room, leaving a man in his dressing gown on the bed. He is watching TV.

I've seen hundreds. And all with different people.

Joanna gets in bed and lies next to him. He is oblivious to her presence. The film is Brief Encounter. *It is nearing the end. We do not see the film, but we do hear the music and the final scene, and the train. Both Joanna and the man are crying, and sharing handkerchiefs and chocolates though he is unaware of this.*

This is one of my favorites. I love watching the same film in different rooms with different people. People are very beautiful when they watch films, it's like several skins fall away from them.

And then one night as I watched the end of a film with a video distributor from Bristol, it occurred to me that

41

someone might make a film about me, about Thomas and me, and about what happened. And someone might watch it. And I could sit on the end of the bed and watch them watching. Watching my story.

Joanna sits with her baby in silent terror in her cottage. We are in 1350. A dark night. Wind blows. Enter Joanna's mother with a bowl of hot water. Villagers wait around the cottage.

Mother You have to come and eat.

Joanna Don't touch me. Don't come near me.

Mother You have to eat.

Villagers It was three months since the rider had come along the coast. Half the population was dead. But Joanna and her baby Thomas were alive. Because the day Thomas was born, Joanna had sworn to see and touch no one until the plague had lifted its curse.

Joanna Dear Father. I trust that you would not bring Thomas into this world only to kill him with such pain. I have faith that you are not cruel, and that Thomas's birth is a blessing on this house.

Villagers Joanna and Thomas had barricaded themselves into a small room at the back of her family's hut. Even her husband was not allowed in. One day her mother came to the door to say that her husband had died. She barely reacted. Days passed. Weeks. Her brother died. Her father. Still she maintained her vigil.

Mother How can you feed the baby if you don't eat?

Joanna Where did the food come from?

Mother From the ground, where d'you think?

Joanna Who picked it? Who washed it?

Mother I did.

Joanna Where did you go today?

Mother I went to market.

Joanna Stay at the door!

Mother You have to eat.

Villagers But she didn't. She didn't eat, and she only drank water that she herself raised from the well at night. She knew that her milk would soon run dry, and that her baby may starve. Rather that than the agony of the plague.

Joanna (*kneels in prayer*) Dear God, save me from my sins, protect me from evil, for thine is the kingdom, for ever and ever, amen.

Villagers It was said in the village that Joanna was as close to God as a person could be. That she had a kind of magic in her, a kind of holiness.

Joanna (*praying*) I take succour in the fact that so many who are strong have died but Thomas who is vulnerable is still alive. I have faith that his weakness is his strength and that you have cast your mercy upon his soul. I have faith that you have not forsaken us.

Villagers And so it seemed. The deaths in the town started to slow. From one a day to one a week. One a month. Then nothing. Joanna's milk had run dry and her baby fed only on water from the well. It was the day of St Christopher.

Mother It's morning.

Joanna Has anyone died in the night?

Mother It is three months since anyone died.

Joanna What kind of day is it?

Mother It's a bright sunny day. St Christopher's Day.

Pause.

Joanna I will eat with you tonight.

They hug, the mother holds the baby. A feast is prepared of meats and vegetables.

Villager That night they ate like kings. Friends were invited. People of the town.

A group of revellers join together.

The many deaths meant that there was more food to go round. Vegetables, bread, even a slice of meat. Joanna ate until she could eat no more. And they danced.

A dance. It is vibrant and joyous, the baby passed from person to person.

It was a dance of joyous, ecstatic life. Joanna said to herself –

Joanna Happiness like this has never existed until now.

Villager (*pause*) But as they danced . . . Death entered the room. Joanna felt it and saw it, but no one else noticed.

Death enters and, circling the oblivious dancers, embraces the mother. Joanna stares in fear. The mother is unaware of his embrace. Suddenly, and while holding the baby, the mother starts to reel, her dance changing shape to a dance of death, as she clutches at her throat and her groin.

Joanna No. No!

Joanna pulls her child from her mother but the mother resists, helped by Death itself.

Give him to me!

The mother is starting to foam at the mouth. Blood is pouring from her mouth. She splutters, she reels, she

releases the baby, she laughs wildly, she twitches, she
collapses. Joanna flees with her child.

Villager Joanna returned to the darkness of her room.
But in her heart she knew it was too late.

Joanna sits holding her baby.

That night, Joanna did not pray.

Joanna The plague cares not for prayers. It has killed
those who prayed and spared those who did not. It has
taken children and spared tyrants. It has no interest in
good or evil. So what is the point of being good? What
is the point of praying?

Villager And Joanna challenged God in a voice of
defiance and rage.

Joanna You have taken my father and mother. You have
taken my husband. You may take my sister and my
friends and everyone I know upon this earth. But you
will not take my child! Promise me you will not take my
child or I will curse you to the depths of hell!

Villager But, Joanna, there was only silence, as if God
had deserted her to the spirit of death.

Joanna Promise me!

Villagers The more she exhorted, the darker and more
silent the night became. And Joanna cast her eyes away
from God and was filled with the fury of the devil.

Joanna I hate you. I curse you. You shan't take him.
I won't let you! He has not lived to die like that! (*to
baby*) You haven't lived to die like that!

*Joanna looks at her baby and slowly starts to stroke
its face. She unwinds the blanket from its tiny body,
and pressing it on to the baby's face, she suffocates
her child.*

45

Silence.

Villager When the struggle was over, Joanna sat and listened to the silence. It occurred to her that even the birds had died.

Joanna Death. If you are here now, listen to me. I want to die. I want to die.

NINE: NOT SEEING IS BELIEVING

The hotel room has returned to its modern form and Francis is listening to Joanna in her hotel maid's uniform.

Joanna I want to die.

Francis What do you mean, you want to die?

Joanna What I say.

Francis You mean you have a death wish?

Joanna If you like.

Francis Have you ever tried to . . . I mean, have you ever attempted . . .

Joanna I can't.

Francis Who knows about this? Your family?

Joanna I have none.

Francis Listen. You need to get help.

Joanna That's what I'm doing now.

Francis No, I mean professional help. Counselling. There are people who are trained.

Joanna That won't work with me.

Francis Everyone says that at first, but the fact is . . . everyone has tough times, we've all been there.

Sometimes you get through it yourself, sometimes you need someone to talk to, to bounce off. Someone who understands.

Joanna Don't you understand?

Francis I do up to a point. But I'm not qualified to help you. I can tell you what sorbet you want. You need proper medical help.

Joanna I thought you liked talking to me.

Francis I know people. I can get you some numbers.

Joanna Numbers are no use to me.

Francis Maybe I could help you out. I mean these people aren't cheap.

Joanna I don't want your money.

Francis You need to talk to someone!

Joanna I'm talking to you!

Pause.

You don't want me here any more.

Francis That's not true.

Joanna You just wanted to sleep with me.

Francis That's not true.

Joanna Then help me!

Francis What do you want from me?

Joanna If I tell you, you won't believe me.

Francis How do you know that?

Joanna You'll leave. I know you will.

Francis I won't leave. I promise.

Joanna But you don't understand. If you leave . . .

Francis I won't leave.

Joanna I can't take it any more. I can't go back, not now I know what's it's like . . .

Francis Joanna. I swear. I won't leave.

Joanna Touch me. Touch my face. Please.

Pause. He touches her face.

Touch my body.

Francis I don't think . . .

Joanna Do it.

He does so.

The reason I'm speaking to you, and no one else, is that you are the only person who can do that.

Francis Do what?

Joanna See me. Hear me. Feel me.

Francis Excuse me?

Joanna I'm invisible to everyone except you.

Francis You mean the real you is invisible to most people.

Joanna No, I mean I'm invisible.

Francis (*smiles*) You mean literally?

Joanna Yes.

Pause.

I knew you wouldn't believe me.

Francis laughs.

Francis What do you mean? You mean other people can't see you?

Joanna You're getting the idea now.

Francis Wh–wh–what are you saying?

Joanna I'm a spirit.

Francis Oh, great.

Joanna I know.

Francis Oh, you really are nuts. That's fantastic. And whence do you hail?

Joanna The fourteenth century.

Francis Oh excellent, one of my favourites. You're right, I don't believe you.

Joanna I know.

Francis I should never do one-night stands. Help me out. This is a bit of fun. You're having a bit of fun.

Joanna Believe me, I'd much rather sleep with you, but it's coming between us, you see.

Francis Any particular reason why the fourteenth century?

Joanna I didn't have a choice.

Francis Listen, you may think you're from the fourteenth century. Which for you means that you do, I know. But that still leaves the question why.

Joanna You think I'm psychopathological.

Francis You're definitely psycho-something.

Joanna A psychopathologist from Stirling stayed here two years ago. I read some of his papers.

Francis And?

Joanna He had a threesome with two waitresses from a bar by the harbour.

Francis Listen, I don't have time for this. I have a funeral tomorrow, I have to look at the speech . . .

Joanna I was born early in the fourteenth century in a small cottage about half a mile from here.

Francis I don't want to hear it.

Joanna I had three brothers and a sister. In what I now believe to be 1350 . . .

Francis I don't want to hear it. You're delusional. You need help. I will help you as much as I can but I have my own problems to deal with.

Joanna What are you doing?

Francis I'm giving you some money.

Joanna Put it away.

Francis I'm offering you money so you can solve your problem!

Joanna I don't want your money! You think money can solve everything, well, it will do nothing for me! (*Pause.*) Why don't we forget the whole thing?

Francis I didn't mean to laugh at you.

Joanna No, you're probably right.

Francis It's not a question of being right.

Joanna No, you are.

Francis I know why you were in the bathroom. It was a cry for help. I understand. And I like you, Joanna. I really do. But this is a bad time for me.

Joanna Can I buy you a drink in the bar to make up for it?

Francis I don't know if that's sensible.

Joanna One drink. And I promise I will talk to whomever you recommend me to talk to.

Francis One drink.

Joanna One drink.

They leave the room and enter the lift . . . the lift descends . . .

This has been a particularly stressful day for me.

Francis And not just you.

. . . they take the lift to the foyer.

Joanna By the way. Did the girl on the desk really not know me?

Francis No, she'd never heard of you.

Joanna Could you introduce me?

Francis You work in the same hotel and you want me to introduce you?

Joanna I'm a bit shy. I think if I had a few more friends here . . .

Francis All right, if it will help.

Tracy is at the desk, head down.

Excuse me?

Tracy Yes, how may I be of assistance to you, sir?

Francis I just wanted to clear something up. I asked you on the phone about a maid called Joanna. You said there was no one of that name working here.

Tracy That's correct, sir. I make it my business to get to know all of the staff personally and I can assure you we have no one of that name.

Francis Well, may I introduce Joanna. (*Beat.*) Recognise her now?

  Pause.

Tracy Oh, very funny, sir. Very good.

Francis What is?

Tracy I don't know. Is it meant to be funny?

Francis I'm just introducing you, that's all I'm doing. Joanna, this is Tracy. Tracy, this is Joanna.

Joanna Hello, Tracy.

Francis Tracy? Joanna just said hello.

Tracy Am I missing something, sir?

Francis What is wrong with everyone in this hotel? I'm asking you a very simple question: have you ever seen this girl before? And if not, then shouldn't you get to know each other?

Tracy You're scaring me now.

Francis Why am I scaring you?

Tracy Well, what girl do you mean?

Francis What girl? This girl. This girl standing here!

Tracy There is no girl.

  Pause.

Joanna I'm sorry. I knew no other way.

  Blackout.

Act Two

ONE: A SICK JOKE

Midnight in the hotel. Tracy is at reception, looking bored and doing her nails. Terry enters in night-watchman uniform, wet.

Terry The midnight hour approacheth. Which means my shift.

Tracy How are you, Terry?

Terry Tremendous, thank you.

Tracy How's the training?

Terry Ran two miles today.

Tracy Did you run them all in one go?

Terry Not strictly, no.

Tracy Can I be honest, Terry? Unless you muscle down to some serious application, your marathon is going to remain a pipe dream in your head. There's a towel. (*Hands him a towel.*) Bottom line, you're not running twenty-six miles until you start taking your challenges seriously.

Terry Yeah well . . .

Tracy I don't mean to be harsh.

Terry No, fair dos.

Tracy And you don't look tremendous. You look woeful.

Terry To be honest, it's not been a majorly good day. Landlord's hiked the rent. Says what with the prices going through the roof, he could get twice as much as

I'm paying. Where am I going to live, I says? Not my problem, he says. And when you look at it, it isn't. I could be freezing to death under the pier and at the end of the day it's not his problem. You know whose problem it is?

Tracy It's yours, Terry.

Terry In one! Then, on the course of my run, I bump into this bloke I was at school with. We weren't close or anything but we weren't distant. Anyway, he remembers, after a bit of jogging, jogging of the memory kind I mean, and he tells me he's staying at the Phoenix, so we arrange to have a little drink, wander down memory lane and all that. Long story short, I get to the Phoenix, it's pissing with rain, I've soaked my best suit, and the bastard's not even staying there. I mean, what's all that about?

Tracy He probably didn't want to see you.

Terry Well, the thought did occur to me. He's done all right for himself, that's what it is. Doesn't want to be seen with the likes of me.

Tracy That's probably it.

Terry Thanks for the moral support, Trace.

Tracy Terry, there's no good comes from delusions. I could say, oh, maybe he got the name of the hotel wrong, but that would most likely be a lie wouldn't it? (*Beat.*) You need a good laugh to cheer you up.

Terry Last time I laughed, you were a twinkle in the milkman's.

Tracy I've got just the thing.

Terry I doubt it. I may laugh politely, but a real belly laugh. The odds aren't strong.

54

Tracy You listen to this. It was just before eleven. The lift opens.

The lift opens. It is Francis. He is behaving strangely, in that he is talking as before to Joanna, but Joanna is not there. He approaches Tracy.

Francis Excuse me?

Tracy Yes, how may I be of assistance to you, sir?

Francis I just wanted to clear something up. I asked you on the phone about a maid called Joanna. You said there was no one of that name working here.

Tracy That's correct, sir. I make it my business to get to know all of the staff personally and I can assure you we have no one of that name.

Francis Well, may I introduce Joanna.

Pause.

Recognise her now?

Pause.

Tracy Oh, very funny, sir. Very good.

Francis What is?

Tracy I don't know. Is it meant to be funny?

Francis I'm just introducing you, that's all I'm doing. Joanna, this is Tracy. Tracy, this is Joanna.

Pause.

Tracy? Joanna just said hello.

Tracy Am I missing something, sir?

Francis What is wrong with everyone in this hotel? I'm asking you a very simple question: have you ever seen this girl before? And if not, then shouldn't you get to know each other?

55

Tracy You're scaring me now.

Francis Why am I scaring you?

Tracy Well, what girl do you mean?

Francis What girl? This girl. This girl standing here!

Tracy There is no girl.

Pause.

Francis If this is some kind of sick joke . . .

Tracy I don't make jokes. It's not something I do.

Pause.

Francis Can I just say I don't find this remotely amusing. (*to thin air*) You set this up from the very beginning, didn't you? . . . Hiding in my fucking bathroom. Well, let me tell you I don't find it funny in the least. You don't seriously expect me to believe that? I want the manager. You two may think this is very humorous, taking the piss out of a man on the day before his father's funeral . . . No, I will not come back upstairs . . .

A guest arrives through the entrance to check in, a woman in a big coat, an American, fifty.

American I'd like to check in. The name is Wassermann

Tracy Certainly.

Francis Excuse me. I know this is a ridiculous thing to ask, but – (*indicating thin air*) can you see this woman? (*to thin air*) You shut up, I've heard enough from you. (*to Wassermann*) Well? Can you see her, yes or no?

Pause.

Tracy There's your key, Mrs Wassermann, it's first floor on your left.

Francis Excuse me, I asked you a question. Can you see this woman?

56

Mrs Wassermann What the hell do you think you're playing at?

Francis Just tell me you can see her! Tell me! This woman here!

Francis grabs the woman and points her at thin air.

Mrs Wassermann Get your hands off me!

Tracy Sir, I must ask you to refrain from molesting a fellow guest.

Francis I asked her a question! I asked you a question!

Mrs Wassermann There's no one there, and you damn well know there isn't.

Enter suddenly more guests from the bar. A party of conferencees, all a bit drunk and flirty.

Francis Wait. All of you stop right there! Now listen to me. Is there or is there not a young woman in chambermaid's uniform standing right here beside me!?

Pause.

Mrs Wassermann You should get some sleep, young man.

Francis What is this? Is this some kind of sick game? Where are the cameras?

He stares wildly, looking for cameras. Then he tries to feel for microphones on Mrs Wassermann's body.

Mrs Wassermann What the hell are you doing?

Francis Where is it? The microphone, where is it? Is this one of those television shows because if it is, you have chosen the wrong man at the wrong time!

Mrs Wassermann screams. Tracy and the conferencees fight Francis off.

The lift doors open. Now Francis falls silent. In the lift he can see Joanna, in rags, carrying a baby. She stares at him silently.

Oh no. Oh no.

He runs into the lift and the doors close.
    Tracy turns to Terry. Terry is laughing.

Terry I have to say. That is choice. Oh dear. Ha ha ha. Oh dear. Where is the poor bastard now?

TWO: STAY

Back in the room. Francis sits on the bed in shocked, stony silence. Enter Joanna as before, in rags, carrying the baby.

Joanna It was just as I'd imagined. I told him my story like a movie. And I didn't stop until I reached the end.

    1350. Night. Joanna is smothering her child in the blanket. Then silence.

Villager When the struggle was over, Joanna sat and listened to the silence. It occurred to her that even the birds had died.

Joanna Death. If you are here now, listen to me. I want to die.

    Joanna feels the skin rip out from under her arms, and her groin, and her tongue rattles like a snake in her throat. She enters the spasms of the plague.

Thank you.

    Her uncle hears her moans and enters the room. He sees the dead baby, and the dying Joanna.

Uncle I'm fetching the priest.

Joanna No! No priest.

Uncle You must confess your sins.

Joanna I don't want a priest! I can't have a priest!

Uncle exits.

Take me, Death! Let me die before he comes!

A shadow at the entrance to the room. A priest enters.

Priest Please leave me with her so I can hear her confession.

He approaches Joanna, who backs away from him in terror. He speaks gently and with compassion.

Joanna? Why do you flee from God's mercy? You have nothing to be afraid of. If any sin weighs on your soul that may impede your passage to heaven, all you have to do is to confess it and Christ in his mercy will bear it for you as he died to bear all our sins. You will join your innocent child, who is already in God's embrace. Tell me now and all is forgiven.

Joanna shakes her head.

You must tell me. Anything. If you missed prayers. If you ever felt anger or lustful desire, or jealousy, tell me and I will receive your confession.

Joanna shakes her head.
Death enters at the door.

I ask you for the third time, if there is any sin in your soul, confess it that you may be redeemed. You have to talk to me. Your soul is at stake. Confess, Joanna! Confess!

Death approaches Joanna and lays his hand upon her. She shakes her head, and in a wail of grief, collapses into his arms. A wild spasm of pain rips through her and she dies.
The Priest hangs his head. The uncle enters.

Uncle Is she dead?

Priest She confessed nothing.

Uncle Perhaps the pain was too much for her.

Priest Perhaps.

Uncle I knew her. She was a good Christian.

Priest Yes, of course.

From all corners of the darkness come the figures. They cover Joanna and Thomas. They process to the burial ground. They lower the bodies into the open trench, and chant the Requiem: 'Requiem eternam dona eis Domine.' God grant them eternal rest.

Suddenly Joanna's body shakes and screams. The figures scatter in terror. The sheet on her body blows away on the wind. Joanna lies there in torments.

The year 2001. In the room Francis is sitting in shock. He suddenly starts to pack everything into his suitcase.

Joanna What are you doing? Where are you going?

Francis I'm moving.

Joanna Where?

Francis To another hotel.

Joanna You can't.

Francis Watch me.

Joanna I won't let you.

Francis Get out of my way.

Joanna No.

Francis Get away from me!

He pushes her. She falls. He grabs his bag and heads for the door. She goes after him and grabs him.

Joanna Francis, wait. Please. You don't know what it means to be here with you. Don't leave me alone. I beg you.

Francis and Joanna grapple at the door.

Francis Why can I see you?

Joanna I don't know.

Francis Why me?

Joanna I don't know.

Francis I don't believe you.

Joanna I didn't choose you.

Francis You don't exist! You're a delusion, a manifestation . . .

Joanna Feel me. I'm warm. I'm real. (*Beat.*) I can't leave the hotel's grounds. If you go, I can't follow you. I'll never see you again.

Francis I need to talk to someone. I need help.

Joanna What are you going to say? Excuse me, I'm with a spirit, how should I proceed?

Francis I'm going to say that I'm going out of my fucking mind!

Joanna Stay with me for one night. One night!

He throws her off. But she returns to grab him again. He throws her off. But she returns and grabs him again. He throws her off. But she returns and grabs him again. He throws her off. But she returns and grabs him again. He throws her off. But she returns and grabs him again. He throws her off. But she returns and grabs him again.

He does not throw her off. She clings to him. She drags him to the mirror. In the mirror he and we can see only himself. She is not there.

One night. That's all I ask.

Francis walks back into the room and hangs his suit back on the hook.

Francis I need a drink.

Joanna What would you like?

Francis Anything.

Joanna pours. He drinks it in one.

Another.

Joanna Gin or Martini?

Francis Both.

She opens the minibar, pours them into one glass.

I'm going tomorrow after the funeral.

Joanna I know.

Francis I have a focus group in Birmingham.

Joanna I know.

Francis I have my life to lead.

Joanna I know.

Francis I have a wife and child!

Pause.

Joanna You have a child?

Francis Yes.

Joanna Boy or girl?

Francis I have a son.

Joanna What's his name?

Francis His name. His name is Thomas.

She gives him the drink, he downs it.

(*to us*) It was then the memory came to me. A few weeks ago. I had driven to Swindon. Another pitch. Another hotel. Another night of thinking about Estelle in another man's bed, and how I didn't really care. Another night thinking of Thomas. I drove back at dawn. The motorway was empty. I have an Audi. I was going fast. I shut my eyes and counted to ten. I wanted to crash. I didn't want to die. I wanted to be pulled from the wreckage. I thought that maybe if by a miracle, a one in a million, I was rescued, then I could start again. I could feel life for the first time. But when I opened my eyes, nothing had happened. Just straight road.

THREE: A DISTANT LIGHT, DANCING

There is a knock at the door. Francis goes to the door, opens it. It is Liz, in an overcoat, soaked through.

Liz It's late. I shouldn't have come.

Francis Wait there for a second. (*Francis runs back in, grabs his coat.*) My sister.

Joanna Let her in.

Liz (*entering*) Are you with someone?

Francis No!

Pause. She sees that he is alone.

Liz I couldn't sleep. All these thoughts . . .

Francis Listen, why don't we go for a walk?

Liz It's raining. (*Beat.*) Have you been drinking?

Francis A little. What about the bar?

Liz It's shut.

*Liz takes off her coat and scarf and sits on the bed.
She does not see Joanna. But she does see the second
glass.*

You've had someone in here.

Francis I used two glasses, that's all.

Liz She's not in the bathroom, I hope. That would be too
much of a cliché.

Pause.

(*seeing the black suit*) Nice suit. Brand new, isn't it?

Francis Marks and Spankers. They happened to have my
size. Can I get you anything?

Liz No thanks.

Francis How long has it been raining?

Liz Quite a while. The brolly was in Mum's room, I didn't
want to wake her.

Francis When did you move back in?

Liz When Vince left. I was broke. It was a short-term
solution. Six years.

Francis Has it been all right?

Liz No, it's been living hell, since you ask.

Pause.

What are you going to do, Frank?

Francis About what?

Liz About world famine. What do you think?

Francis I don't want to talk about that now.

Liz I had no idea this was going to happen. And when
you left, I had such a go at Mum. I was going to make
her come over here and take it back.

64

Joanna Take what back?

Liz At first she wouldn't say anything. She sat at the kitchen table, we both just sat there. And then, I don't remember exactly when, she started crying. I couldn't stop her. It was like a dam breaking. She told me about the time Dad got laid off at the docks. She did everything. She worked down the electric works, came home, cooked for us, washed us, put us to bed, cooked for him, washed up, put him to bed. Every day the same. Four years. She said the thing what kept her going was knowing what a wonderful son she had. You were a hard-working little bastard, remember? God, I hated you. Then things got better. Dad got work delivering barrels. You did well at school. I was a mess but that didn't really matter. And when you and Dad had the argument, she wasn't worried. She didn't think it would last. It was only a fight. Every year, Christmas was the main time, she'd think, this'll be the year. He'll just turn up at the door. And then, on the fifth year you didn't come, she said to Dad: 'Shame Frank isn't here.' Dad didn't even answer. From that moment she started to hate Dad. She hated him until the day he died. And when he was dying she hated herself for hating him; she thought she'd killed him with her hate. So she called you on the telephone, she got your message service. I didn't know she called you, Frank. She went behind my back and she begged you to come and see him. But you didn't come. You didn't even answer her call.

Joanna But you did. Tell her you did.

Liz So then she said, she was stirring her tea very slowly, I made her a tea to try and calm her down, she said, 'If he doesn't give that speech, I'll kill myself.' I don't know if she meant it, but I thought you ought to know.

Pause.

I'll be going now.

Francis No, stay.

Liz No, I'd rather go.

Francis Have a drink.

Liz I'm not having a drink in here. Look at this place! How could you stay here and not in your own house?

Francis I just couldn't.

Liz I've spent six years in that place and you couldn't even manage one night!

Francis I'm sorry.

Liz I worshipped you! I knew I was nothing compared to you, but I'm still here, dealing with the shit you left behind. It's not fair! So you know what you're going to do? You're going to read that speech she wrote. You're going to read it with tears in your eyes. You're not going to do it for her or for him, or for yourself. You're going to do it for me. Because you owe me.

Francis Liz, wait.

Liz Don't touch me.

Francis Let me get you a taxi at least.

Liz I don't want a fucking taxi!

She leaves, slamming the door behind her. Joanna goes over to the suit and takes out the speech. She reads it.

Joanna (*to us*) As I read the speech again, I felt a veil lift from the events of that night. I glimpsed for the first time the possibility of redemption. It was distant, like a tiny dancing light seen from a hill. You don't quite know how far away it is. And at any minute as you approach, it may flicker and die.

Francis This has nothing to do with you.

Joanna What are you going to do?

Francis I don't know.

Joanna Are you going to read this?

Francis It seems that's what everyone wants.

Joanna You like giving people what they want.

Francis What does that mean?

Joanna In the women's magazines in the foyer, that's all they talk about: 'Getting what you want from your life.' What do you want, Francis?

Francis I want this all to be over.

Joanna Why didn't you answer her call?

Francis I meant to. I was busy.

Joanna What did he do that could have been so bad?

Francis I told you. This has nothing to do with you.

Joanna You tried to sleep with me on the back of that speech.

Francis I need another aspirin.

Joanna A speech you never wrote.

   Pause.

Francis It was a disagreement.

Joanna What about?

Francis He'd lost his job. Mum was away, he got drunk, I mean he got drunk. And he just started laying into me. Like it was my fault. Saying I'd betrayed him, saying I was a Judas. And then, he was taking a sip of beer and suddenly he just went at me. He hit me and kicked me.

I didn't react. I just let him do it. I just remember saying, 'That's right old man, let it all out. Let it all out.'

Pause.

Joanna And you left.

Francis The same night.

Joanna You could never forgive him?

Francis Judas doesn't forgive.

Pause.

Joanna And that's it?

Francis What else should there be?

Joanna I don't understand.

Francis What is there to understand?

Joanna But it's not possible.

Francis I'm telling you that's what happened.

Joanna No, Francis. That is not what happened!

Pause.

Come with me.

Francis Where?

Joanna Come on.

Francis Where are we going?

They leave the room and enter the lift.

Francis Where are we going?

Joanna Down.

The lift descends beyond the ground floor to the basement.

Francis (*to us*) Down. Down where? I should have taken that aspirin. My breath was short. My head. I knew what it was. It's a kind of mini-breakdown, stress-induced, you read about it, it's the effect of too much travel, too many nights alone in air-conditioned rooms, no one really knows the effect of that processed air, and the light, the fluorescent, the flicker as you enter, no one knows the effect of the TV, the way the channels change, the strange sudden fade to black and then up, another image, a crocodile, a remote mountain outpost, reddibrek, guerrillas with Nikes, Ronny Corbett, Rwanda, black girls in bikinis, drive-by shootings, down up down up down . . .

FOUR: THE BURIAL GROUND

The lift doors open. They are in a dark space. Black soil. Crosses. Stones. Darkness. Francis follows Joanna out. Joanna turns on a torch.

Francis What are we doing here?

Joanna Come.

Francis What is this?

Joanna They planned it as a basement for the laundry rooms but it was never built. When they started digging the foundations, they found it.

Francis Found what?

Joanna Bits of bones and skulls, most had rotted away, mainly teeth remained. They didn't tell anyone because they knew they wouldn't be allowed to continue and the loss on the project would have been substantial. But the idea of having the laundry down here didn't seem right. So they left it just as they found it.

Pause.

For four hundred years this was my home.

*Joanna walks across the black soil in despair. Her head
tries to rise to heaven but is pulled down by the weight
of her sin.*

After the plague, no one came near the burial ground.
I was alone, no one to talk to, no one to look at. This
was my hell. Then one night I saw him.

*The soul of a child floats over the burial ground. A
boy.*

Child Mama?

Joanna Thomas? Is that you? Thomas! Where are you?

Child I am in paradise, Mama.

Joanna Can I touch you?

Child No, Mama. Your sin stops you touching me. You
look sad.

Joanna Do I?

Child I'm sorry you're sad.

Joanna You make me happy being here.

Child I'm happy too. But I have to go soon.

Joanna Can you visit me again?

Child I'm sorry, Mama. I'm not allowed any more.

Joanna Can't you ask to come once more?

Child It's not allowed. I have to tell you something.
There is a way for you to be with me.

Joanna How?

Child Another will come. A man who has lost his faith.
Who has not confessed his sin. You must stop him

making the mistake you made. You must save him. Then you will save yourself. And we will be together again.

Joanna When will he come?

Child He will come.

Joanna But how will I know? How will I know it is him?

Child He will see you. I have to go now.

Joanna No, Thomas, please don't go.

The child disappears.

Thomas? Thomas!!! (*Pause. To Francis*) Time passed. No one came. The land stayed derelict and forgotten. The bones decayed and disappeared. I lost hope, decided it was just another torture, a devil tormenting me for my crime. Then they built the paper mill. Men worked at the machines. Real skin and muscle. My heart soared. But none of them saw me. Then it closed. Only a few kids breaking in to smash the old machinery. Then, suddenly, the ring road, the hotel. Then you. You saw me.

Joanna stares at him.

Francis It's nothing to do with me.

Joanna If he wronged you, what have you to confess?

Francis I told you, you've got the wrong person.

Joanna Francis, sometimes I hear thoughts. After I asked you to stay, you sat down on the bed and you had a drink, a Martini and gin. You stayed silent for a long time.

Francis So?

Joanna What were you thinking?

Francis I can't remember.

Joanna You were thinking about how a few weeks ago you had driven to Swindon to do a pitch. Another hotel. Another night of thinking about your wife in another man's bed, and how you didn't really care. Another night thinking of Thomas. You drove back at dawn. You have an Audi. You were going fast. You shut your eyes and counted to ten. You wanted to crash. You didn't want to die. You wanted to be pulled from the wreckage. You thought maybe if you were rescued by a miracle, a one in a million, then you could start again. You could feel life for the first time.

Pause.

Francis How did you know that?

Joanna If you were so wronged by your father, why is it you that needs to be saved?

Francis I don't.

Joanna Why do you need to start again? Why do you not feel life?

Francis I do.

Joanna Why do you not care that your wife is having an affair? Why do you not defend yourself?

Francis I do.

Joanna She might be with him now. Why don't you care?

Francis I'm warning you . . .

Joanna Why don't you care about anything? The money you make, it should bring you happiness, but it doesn't. Why not? (*Beat.*) Why when you kiss do your lips feel cold?

Francis I don't know what you're saying.

Joanna Why can't you kiss? Why can't you give yourself even to that?

Francis I can!

Joanna Why can't you feel?

Francis I can feel!

Joanna Show me.

Francis All right. I will. I'll fucking show you!

Francis kisses her, grapples with her, strangles her, physical, violent. Then he stops, forlorn, in her arms.

Joanna I will save you. Just tell me what from.

FIVE: THE SECRET TO ETERNAL LIFE

In the hotel foyer, Terry is reading a book called How to Live Forever *and is on the phone.*

Terry *How to Live Forever.* It is catchy, yeah. It's all about organ regeneration. Listen to this, Mum, this is the back cover: 'Ours is the first generation in human history that has the technological ability to regenerate our own bodies. Now Dr Judith Klitzer, one of the world's leading experts in genetic engineering, gives you the secrets to eternal life. Which organs die first? Which last longest? And how much will you need to spend to become immortal?' About twenty million, she reckons. Well, let's hope it's dollars for our sake. Listen, it's quarter to five, you should get some sleep. I'll be with you about eight, same as every morning. Mum, I told you, no fry-ups. How am I going to be immortal if I have a full English every bloody morning? I love you too. Course I do. Sweet dreams.

He puts the phone down, turns on some black-and-white screens. He can see the corridors of the hotel. They are all empty. The bar. Empty. Then he stops dead. In the basement, he can see a figure standing. It is Francis and he is talking to thin air.

Fuck me.

He stands and ambles to the lift, and enters.
  In the basement Francis pauses. The lift descends.
Terry enters with a large torch. Joanna immediately
puts hers out.

Hello? Who's there?

His beam alights on Francis.

Bloody hell.

Francis Hello, Terry.

Joanna (*to Francis*) Don't look at me.

Terry whizzes his beam around the room but does not
see Joanna.

Terry You alone?

Francis Yes.

Terry Listen, I don't want to pry, but may I ask what
you're doing? It's just this area is out of bounds. You
can't get to it without a special key and all that.

Francis I got the wrong floor. It was open.

Terry It's that ditzy bloody girl again. I'll have to have
words. I saw you on the screen. You looked like you
were talking to someone.

Francis Did I?

Joanna (*to Francis. Terry can't hear*) What's wrong?

Francis Nothing.

Terry What's that?

Francis Nothing. I owe you an explanation.

Terry Yes, I went to the Phoenix as per the arrangement.

Francis I checked out.

Terry You didn't really check in, did you? Listen, if you don't want to see me, that's your right, but I'd rather you didn't lie.

Francis Sorry.

Terry I may not be the first name in your address book, but there are still ways of behaving.

Francis It's my father's funeral tomorrow.

Terry Your father? Well, why didn't you say so?

Francis I don't know. I was confused.

Terry Good man, your dad. He gave me a penny once. Big old one it was. You speaking at the funeral?

Francis Yes. Yes, I am.

Terry That's nice. I spoke at my father's. Very poignant occasion. Listen, are you all right? I'm just beginning to put two and two together, and it seems to me it was probably you what Tracy spoke to earlier, about the 'girl'?

Francis Oh that. That was a misunderstanding.

Terry Have you been drinking, Frank? I mean it's none of my business, but if you're giving the oration . . .

Francis I'm fine. I am sorry about the Phoenix.

Terry It's just I suddenly thought that you never liked me and I remember you very fondly.

Francis You too.

Terry I remember when my old man died. It's like someone takes away your legs and tells you to walk twice as fast as before. (*Beat.*) I'm going to have to ask you to come out of here.

Francis Yes, of course.

They enter the lift.

Terry Speaking of your dad, I found out more about that McGeechan fellow. He left a suicide note. Would you believe it? He's still denying he ever killed your dad's dog.

Pause.

Francis Don't remember much about it.

Terry Twenty years later it must be, he tops himself, and he's still going on about that bleeding bloody dog.

Joanna suddenly pushes the emergency stop button on the lift.

Terry What happened?

Francis We've stopped. Let me just . . .

He flicks it back on but Joanna flicks it back off.

Terry What you up to?

Francis Nothing.

Joanna Ask him about the dog. Ask him.

Terry How are we going to get out of here?

Francis Can't we hit the alarm?

Terry If you hit the alarm, it goes to the desk, which is where I'm meant to be. I'm going to get done for this. I'm not supposed to use the lifts. I'm supposed to walk.

Joanna Ask him.

Pause.

Francis Did McGeechan say anything in the note?

Terry Just said it wasn't him that did it. I mean the police never proved it anyway. It was only rumour. But he was a bit simple, that was the thing. Couldn't get over the shame. People looking at him funny in the street. Saying things. Couldn't cope with it, poor bastard. Well, it's all ancient history now.

Joanna clicks the button, and the lift rises.

We're off again. The gremlins in this place, I tell you.

It reaches the ground floor.

Listen, good luck with the speech tomorrow. I hope it isn't too painful for you.

Francis Goodbye, Terry.

Terry And Frank. Look after yourself.

The doors close and Terry wanders back to his desk. On the screen, he sees Francis exiting the lift and walking fast along the corridor, still in animated conversation with thin air.

Poor bastard. The whole thing's got to him.

SIX: LABRADOR

The hotel room. Francis enters followed by Joanna. Francis gets another drink from the minibar. Pause. He stands but is dizzy.

Joanna Are you all right?

Francis I have a headache. I should get ready.

Francis enters the bathroom, turns on the shower. He undresses and enters the shower.

Joanna (*to us*) There's a movie I love. It's only been on once and I've watched out for it since but I've never seen it. A man is playing chess with Death. The man is a knight. He's noble and clever and handsome. He thinks

77

himself more than a match for the hooded figure on the other side of the board. But as the film plays out, you know that there will only be one winner.

Francis comes out of the bathroom in a hotel robe. He sits on the bed and starts to dress.

(*She looks at Francis.*) Neither of us knew whose move it was. At least I was sure it was his. And I think he hoped it was mine.

Francis Get me another drink, would you?

Joanna I'm afraid we're down to tonic. You could order some more from your friend . . .

Francis No, I'll be fine.

Joanna It will be dawn soon.

Francis I haven't eaten a thing all night.

Joanna You could order something.

Francis I'm fine.

Joanna What time is the funeral?

Francis I'm due at the flat at nine. Then we go to the crematorium.

Joanna When do you give the speech?

Francis Just before he's, before he's . . .

Joanna Cremated.

Francis Yes.

Joanna Is there a wake?

Francis In one of the clubs . . . He used to go to this men's club, horrible place, you could still smell the smoke from the war. They've opened it up for us. It's what he wanted. It won't be much. A cup of coffee, glass of whisky or sherry . . .

Joanna For the ladies . . .

Francis That's exactly what he would have said.

Joanna He was a real gentleman.

Francis Yes. He was.

Pause. Francis is dressed now.

My father's life was marooned by delusions.

Joanna What delusions?

Francis The delusion that we live not as individuals but as a society. That as a society we are bound by common rights and common beliefs.

Joanna Such as?

Francis The belief that we care about others as much as ourselves. That we want to do good.

Joanna And we don't?

Francis Of course we don't. Oh, we pay lip service, and if it doesn't hurt us, we'll help out, but life is based on one thing and one thing only: self-interest.

Joanna What does that mean?

Francis It means that you do what suits you best. Not what suits others, the poor, the meek, the lepers or the blind, no, what suits you. You act for your self-interest and I act for mine, and if enough of us agree that one thing serves our self-interest the best, then that's what wins. And most of us will be happy. That's the only good there is. And anybody who pretends otherwise is a liar or a fool.
   And he couldn't see that.

Father enters. Fifty-four but looks older. Tired. Drunk. We are in the flat in 1983. He drinks from a can. Offers one to Francis. Francis accepts. Father downs his and wanders to his chair. The same chair. The same rug.

79

So although he made sure I got educated the way he never did, my education didn't teach me what he wanted me to learn. It taught me what an utter terrible waste his life had been.

I was twenty-four. I'd started a sales business. I was earning in a year more than he could in ten. I'd come down to visit them every now and then for the weekend. He couldn't look at me. We'd end up arguing. If it wasn't for Mum. She loved us both, we didn't want to upset her. One weekend, she had to go and look after her sister. We were alone. I should have left. Some crazy urge kept me there. Like I had business.

He had this dog. It was an old labrador, he'd had it fifteen years, and he loved that dog more than anything. Mum used to say that he loved Trench, that was the dog's name, she used to say he loved Trench more than her. And that Saturday I'd left the door open and Trench had gone walkabout. I mean, he'd done it before, he always came back, but that wasn't the point. The point was I'd left the door open.

That night we got drunk in the flat. I could see from his eyes he was building to something. He was drinking with a purpose.

Father drinks from a can. Gulps.

Father My barrel-lifting days are numbered.

Francis Meaning?

Father Back's gone.

Francis How bad?

Father It's bad. It's bad or I wouldn't be bringing it up.

Francis Can you work?

Father I can work. I can't lift.

Francis But don't you need to lift?

Father Well, I can't, can I? I've lifted for thirty years, as a result of which I cannot lift any more.

Francis What can you do?

Father Make tea? I can't pack it in. We need the money.

Francis She works in the shop.

Father She makes bugger-all working in that shop.

Francis She said she did all right.

Father 'All right.'

Francis You just don't want her supporting you again.

Father What if I don't?

Francis Get with it, Dad. Women can work . . .

Father Her salary doesn't even cover the rent. (*Father gulps.*) I need a job, Francis. One that doesn't mean lifting weights.

Francis Have you looked?

Father I'm fifty-four. My back's shot to pieces. There are three million unemployed. Yes, I've looked.

Francis What you going to do?

Father I don't know. I just thought . . . it's stupid.

Francis What is?

Father I thought you could help me.

Francis What d'you mean?

Father You know. Find me a job.

Francis Where?

Father I don't know. You're doing well.

Francis You mean with me?

Father You're always saying I should keep up with the times. Well, maybe you're right. I've followed what I thought was the right path for a man and look where it's landed me. I've got to change. You've got to help me change, Francis.

Francis Why are you calling me Francis? You never call me Francis.

Pause.

What would you do?

Pause.

Father I can sell things on the phone.

Francis You?

Father Why not? You've just got to have a phone, haven't you? I could do it here. Or I could commute to one of those centres. I can still move.

Francis You're not serious?

Father What d'you mean?

Francis Dad, do you really think you're what I look for? The profile for phone operators is young, mainly women . . .

Father Why?

Francis People trust women.

Father That's all bollocks.

Francis No it isn't.

Father What about selling to old people? If I'm buying something on the phone, I don't want some giggly teenager. I want to hear a voice of experience.

Francis And I want to hear someone who isn't bearing a grudge against mankind.

Father You're not giving me a chance.

Francis I just don't see you as the tele-sales type, that's all.

Father Well something else then. You must need caretakers, night-watchmen.

Francis It's not that kind of business.

Father Well, something else. I'll do anything.

Francis I'm sorry.

Father I need a job. I need a job, do you hear me? I was brought up to work. That is what I do.

Francis What are you, a horse?

   Pause.

They've let you go, haven't they?

Father Given me a month's pay.

Francis Have you told Mum? (*Beat.*) You must get disability benefit.

Father I refused to sign the form.

Francis You what?

Father I'm not disabled! I can work. I've worked all my life, I can work the rest! I just can't lift.

Francis Thing is, Dad – lifting is what you do.

   Pause.

I can give you money. Get you through the next bit.

Father I don't want your money.

Francis Don't be stupid.

Father I don't want your dirty money! I want a job like any man wants a job. I have a right to a job.

Francis No you don't.

Father Listen, you little bastard! I worked to give you everything! Now I want a job so I can look my own wife in the eye . . .

Francis How much do you want?

Father Put that away!

Francis I'm not giving you a fucking job, you dinosaur. Now how much do you want? Five thousand? Ten?

Father I'm no beggar!

Francis I'm not asking you to beg! I'm offering! I'm offering you ten thousand pounds, now stop being so fucking obstinate!

Father I am not your charity case!

Francis I'm writing the cheque.

Father Don't do this, Frank. Have some respect for what I want.

Francis Don't talk to me about respect! You're smashed up, you're stone broke! You're on the slag heap like I always knew you would be! But you wouldn't fucking listen!

Father You can't see! You can't see outside your little tiny bubble!

Francis What does that mean?

Father You think you're so right! Well, maybe you are! You think I wasn't right once? You think I wasn't the man? You think you won't be like me one day . . . trying to keep pace in a world you can't understand and don't care for?

Francis Just take the money. Ten, twenty, I don't care. There. Twenty thousand, which I don't even fucking have. You'll be fine for years with that.

He approaches with the cheque. The father tears it up.
Pause. Francis gets out his cheque book.

OK. I'm going to give you another chance. Now, take the fucking money, and if it makes it easier, I won't tell Mum where it came from. We can pretend you got a payout or something. Now for fuck's sake see some sense.

Francis approaches again. The father tears it up again.

Francis I'm writing you another cheque.

Father Frank, please.

Francis I am writing you another fucking cheque!

Father Frank, don't do this.

Francis writes another cheque.

Francis I am doing it. Thirty thousand. Now you listen to me. This is your last chance. You better fucking take it because I HAVE HAD ENOUGH.

He approaches. Father takes the cheque. Son and father look at each other.

Put the cheque in your pocket. Put it in your pocket. Put it in your pocket!

Pause. Father tears it slowly in half.
Pause. Francis grabs his father by the neck and begins to strangle him. But the father grabs his arms and is stronger than him. They grapple for a while, the father gaining control. He has his son in a lock and is pressing him to the ground.

Father How does it feel? How does it feel!

He releases Francis, who exits and returns with an old golf club. He holds the golf club above his father's head. Father looks at him without moving.

I taught you with that.

Exit Father.

Francis (*to Joanna*) I heard the front door shut. Silence. Something about that look. About what he said. I felt like I was falling through space. Then I heard a scratch at the door. I thought it was him. I ran to open it. This time I was going to really show him.

He runs to the door and opens. It is Trench. (The dog may not actually be there, but he is there for Francis.)

It wasn't him. It was Trench. Stupid beast had found its way home. Hair was hanging off its coat. Bloodshot eyes. And the smell. It ambled into the living room and stood there like a stupid useless beast. And it was my father. My father with four legs and a mangy tail and these fucking doleful I-told-you-so eyes. I took a kick at him. He looked surprised. A bit hurt, what had he done to me? I took another kick. Caught his jaw. He started to snap back at me. Bit me on the ankle. Bit me. I took the golf club and I held it above his head. He just looked at me. I brought it down on his head. I smashed his skull in. Then I smashed his body and his legs and his back, and I kept going until he was a mess of blood and bone on the rug.

Pause.

I left. I went straight to my car and drove the three hours home. I waited in the dark by the phone. I waited for days, don't know how many, skipped work, skipped meals. Then I get a call from my mum.

Enter Doreen on the phone. She is crying.

Doreen Frank? Frank are you there? Pick up the phone. Frank listen. You've got to forgive him for what he did. You've got to come back. I know you said you wouldn't but you've got to.

Francis (*picks up phone*) Forgive him for what?

Doreen For saying what he said. For striking you. He didn't mean it. He was drunk, he didn't know what he was doing. (*Beat.*) Frank, something terrible has happened.

Francis What?

Doreen Trench is dead, Frank. Some bastard beat him to death on the road.

Francis What do you mean?

Doreen The police found him today in some bushes out by the bypass. His skull was smashed in. They've got some bloke in the cells. Who would do such a thing? Frank, Harry said you swore you'd never come back. That's not true, is it? Tell me that's not true, Frank. Frank? Frank!

Francis has hung up. Pause.

Francis (*to Joanna*) Now I understood. He'd covered for me. He'd cleaned the rug, put the dog in the car, driven it out to the ring road and left it there. And the story? It was his way of saying, what happened is between us. Don't tell her. And don't ever come back.

Pause.

Joanna What are you going to say?

Francis What do you mean?

Joanna Which oration are you going to give?

Francis I'm not telling them that.

Joanna You have to.

Francis laughs.

You have to.

Francis Why do you think he did it in the first place? I was everything to that woman. He knew it would kill

87

her to know what I did. He wanted her to believe in me, to be able to come and see me, away from him. But he didn't reckon with her stubbornness. My mother's a purist. If he couldn't see me, nor would she.

Joanna And she never forgave him for that.

Francis If I want to make her happy, I'll give the speech she wrote. That way everybody wins.

Joanna What about your dad?

Francis He's dead.

Joanna How long were they married?

Francis Why?

Joanna How long . . .

Francis Forty-seven. Forty-seven years.

Joanna Is that how you want her to remember him?

Francis You're asking me to destroy myself.

Joanna I'm asking you to close your eyes on the motorway.

Francis Not a day has gone by when I haven't thought about that night. But I've worked hard, I have put my head down and I've worked. I've driven the length and breadth of this country. I've stayed in shithole after shithole seeing no one, talking to no one, doing an empty fucking job for empty fucking people. And I have never once complained because I know that this is my penance. This is my atonement!

Joanna That's not atoning. That's running.

Francis You want me to ruin everything! You want me to tear it all up!

Joanna What are you tearing up?

88

Francis My life! My family! My marriage!

Joanna Is that a marriage?

Francis I'm hanging on by this much! If Estelle finds out, she'll have a reason to leave me. A man who lied and lied to stop his wife learning what he is really like. A man who would willingly let her carry on an affair with his own friend because he thinks he deserves it! And she'll take Thomas with her. You think I'll win custody? A psychopath! He is the only thing I love in the whole world. I will not lose him!

Joanna You are losing him.

Francis I will not lose him!

Joanna You're losing him bit by bit, he's slipping away from you, and you're letting it happen.

  Pause.

You don't know what it would be like with this all over. You don't know what you would be like. You can't remember. You have to take a chance. You have to confess.

Francis I can't do it.

Joanna You can.

Francis I can't.

Joanna I have to see my son!

Francis I can't be left alone.

Joanna You have no idea what loneliness is.

  Pause. Light filters through the window. A solitary bird starts to sing.

Francis (*to us*) I know at this moment I became aware of a bird singing. I know I stayed silent for a long time as the daylight grew into the room. I know that she stood there awaiting my answer. I know that my head throbbed like an accident scene in a film. I know that it suddenly struck me how little you get for your money in hotels like this. That the room is never as big as you would wish. I know that she looked so beautiful standing there, I wanted to make love to her there and then. I know that only then did I realise how many thoughts the human brain can have in one moment. I know that natural light on the face is the most wonderful thing. I know that at some point I got on my knees and blessed God for his creation. I know that I counted the empty bottles from the minibar and there were twelve. I know that I saw Christ. I know that I am mad. I know that I saw him.

The phone rings. Pause.

SEVEN: THE FUNERAL ORATION

Joanna You should answer it.

Francis Hello? Hi, Terry. I slept fine, thank you. They're what? Can you keep them down there? What do you mean they're on their way up?

A rap at the room door. Immediately, Francis and Joanna fly into action, clearing up the room, Francis combing his hair, washing his face, trying to look respectable. A knock at the door again. He opens. His mother and Liz are at the door.

Doreen Thought we'd pick you up.

Pause.

Car's downstairs. You ready?

Francis Just give me a second.

He comes back into the room but the mother follows.

Doreen Roomy. Do you get satellite?

Francis I think so.

Doreen tries the bed.

Doreen Very soft. Where did you sleep?

Francis Shall we . . . .?

Doreen I want you to know something. Lizzie came to see you last night. She shouldn't have done that. What was said was strictly between me and her. I don't want you to do anything for my sake. I want you to do what you think is right.

Francis OK.

Doreen That's what Harry would have wanted. A man like that, his life may not amount to very much, but he has his children. He couldn't forgive himself for what he did. And nor could I. But we both loved you. And I know, in your own way, you loved me, and your dad, and that's all that matters.

Pause.

People never understood Harold. A hundred of them will be there today, and not one of them will understand. They think his life ended in sadness. But I know that somewhere inside, in his soul, he did meet you again, and you did forgive him for what he did, and I know that gave him solace. I could see it in his eyes in his last moments. He was seeing you, Frank, and his eyes were full of softness. So whatever you say, I know what I wrote was true.

Shall we go?

Joanna Don't go yet, Francis.

Doreen I said shall we go?

Joanna Tell her now, and it will make it easier.

91

Doreen Frank?

Liz You all right, Frank?

Joanna Tell her now.

Francis I'm fine.

Joanna Now.

Francis I can't.

Doreen What did you say?

Francis Nothing.

Doreen Can't you find it in your heart to forgive him?

Francis Of course I can.

Doreen Well then.

Joanna Tell her.

Francis (*to Joanna*) Will you shut up?!

   Pause.

Liz Are you all right, Frank?

Francis I didn't sleep very well.

Doreen We'll take you back to our place for a nice breakfast.

Francis What?

Doreen We've got a while before we have to go. Thought it would be nice to have a bit of time with the family. You've not met Harry junior, have you?

Francis Why don't I meet you . . .?

Doreen Liz is doing sausages.

Joanna Don't go.

Doreen Come on or we won't have time.

Joanna She's trying to trap you.

Francis I think it's better if I meet you at the place.

  Pause.

Doreen Do you hate me that much?

Liz Mum.

Doreen Come on, Liz.

Liz Wait, Mum.

Doreen Why can't my son spend an hour with me in my own house!? Am I so appalling?

Liz Mum, please.

Doreen Am I so evil?

Liz (*sudden extreme*) Mum stop it!

Doreen (*to Frank*) Now look what you've done! You've no idea what this girl has suffered on account of you! But you don't care about no one except yourself!

Francis I'll come. I'll come, OK!

Mum I don't want you coming just to please me!

Francis I just said I wanted to!

Mum Don't bother! It's all right, isn't it, Liz? It's not like we're not used to it.

Francis I said I'm coming!

Joanna You've got to tell her now. Please tell her.

Francis I'll do it there.

Doreen What's he saying?

Joanna You have to do it now!

Liz Well, come on then.

Joanna Francis. He was so young when he died. All I've ever thought about is seeing him again.

They go to the door, exit. He draws back.

Francis I've forgotten something. Won't be a moment. (*He runs back in.*) I'm going to tell her. I'm going to tell everyone at the funeral.

Joanna Are you sure?

Francis I have to. I can't live like this any more. I feel so light suddenly. I feel I could take wing. I'm so happy! (*Beat.*) Listen, I have to go.

Joanna Francis. Whatever happens, you won't see me when you get back.

Pause. He holds her. She holds him. He kisses her.

It was warm.

Beat. Then he leaves. Outside the door they walk to the lift.

Doreen I tell you what, Frank. Your old French teacher. Mr Willoughby . . .

Francis What about him?

Doreen He's coming to the funeral. That's nice, isn't it? He always loved you. Wrap up, it's freezing out there.

The lift doors slowly close. Joanna is left alone in the room.

Joanna (*to us*) I like the early mornings. Most of the guests are still asleep. The television's terrible. So I often just lie in an empty room, turn the lights off, and watch the day growing. It's as near as I get to a kind of peace. When I was young, mornings were alive with the throng of the dawn chorus. There was a magnificence in their song, as if they were praising creation itself. Now they

94

grow fewer every year. Sometimes there's just a single sparrow chirping its song. There's a kind of sweetness to that call, you don't know if it's being born or dying.

I listened to the sparrow. I knew I was staring at two doors, one to heaven, one to hell. I suppose that's what purgatory means. You just have to wait for judgement.

Lights fade on Joanna and she disappears into darkness.

Francis enters with a microphone. We are in the crematorium.

Francis Good morning. I'm Francis Chappell. Harold's only son. Forgive me for using a microphone but there are so many of you who have come to pay tribute to Harold, more even than any of us expected, that I do not trust my voice to project what I have to say. I see amongst you some faces I do not know and many faces I do. Faces from my past, faces that have in my absence grown a few wrinkles, heads that have gained a few grey hairs and lost a few brown ones. But I recognise them and I hope they recognise me.

It has fallen to me to give the oration, and there is a reason for that. What I'm going to say will surprise a great deal of you. That I can certainly say is true. It's no secret that many years ago Harold and I had an argument. It's no secret that the argument was serious enough for me to feel it necessary to leave my town and my family, and not come back. This separation has caused a great deal of pain. To myself, and to Harold, of course. But more than that, to my mother, and to my sister Liz. That pain can never be made to disappear. And I feel deep shame for my part . . . for my part . . .

I have here a piece of paper, on which is written a speech. This is. . . . This is what I am to say. It's here. I've had a night to think about it. And at the end of it, as I stand here, before you, I am . . . I'm trying to say that this moment here, this moment in time . . . My

95

mother is looking at me. My beautiful mother. How I missed her. She's smiling. She knows what I'm going to say. Does she know? That smile, that when I was young would comfort me when all around seemed confusion. Is it there to comfort me now? Almost exactly three weeks ago, I was checking my voicemail after, it doesn't matter what it was after. I heard my mother's voice. The voice told me that my father was dying, and it asked me, she asked me to come and see him before he passed away.

This is where the oration begins. Do I read it? What do I say? To you. Friends of Harold. Extended family. Mother. Sister. My judges. Ha ha ha. What do I say? What do I say? The truth. Ah yes. The truth. Well, ladies and gentlemen, the God's honest truth is as follows.

Pause.

Is as follows.

Sudden blackout.
    When the lights come up, the hotel room is empty. We hear the lift ting, and the doors open. Francis comes out, walks along the corridor and into the room. He takes off his black suit and dresses in his ordinary clothes. He packs his bag. He is about to leave.
    A knock at the door. Francis dashes to it at high speed. It is Tracy.

Francis Oh, hello.

Tracy Just to say that checkout is officially at twelve and your room is required by another guest.

Francis Yes, of course. I won't be long. Could you find out the time of the first train to Birmingham?

Tracy You're going to Birmingham?

Francis Yes, I have a focus group.

96

Tracy That's interesting. What's it focusing on?

Francis It's about portals. Mobile phone portals. We're looking at awareness, how aware people are that they exist.

Tracy Very interesting. (*Pause.*) Did events pass as you would have wished? Terry informed me of your loss . . .

Francis Oh yes. Yes thank you.

Tracy I read a book that said it doesn't matter how you live, but only how you die. I think that's very true. Don't you?

  Pause.

Francis I'll be down in a minute.

  He shuts the door. He returns into the room. Pause.

Can you hear me?

  Pause.

If you can, do something. Move some furniture.

  Pause.

Say something. Maybe I can still hear you.

  Joanna enters. Pause. Francis can't see her.

Joanna You can't hear me.

Francis Just say anything. One word.

Joanna One word.

Francis Come on.

Joanna Come on.

Francis Shout. Scream.

  Joanna screams.

Please.

But he can't hear or see her.

You don't know what it was like. You just don't know.

His mobile phone rings. He looks at it, answers.

Hello? Estelle, hi. It went fine. No I don't think I'll be
staying. It just went fine. I told you it went fine. (*Beat.*)
How was your night with Jodie? (*Beat.*) Talk? Why
should we talk? What about? What do you mean, you've
got something to say? (*Pause.*) Yes, let's talk when I get
back, yes. Yes, of course. Yes. Kiss Thomas for me, will
you? Tell him I . . .

*He hangs up. He starts to weep. Joanna holds him
but he can't feel her. For a few seconds his crying is
unrestrained. Then, and almost as suddenly, he pulls
himself together, stands, picks up his stuff and leaves
the room. At the door, he turns.*

If you're there. Trust me. I wasn't the man you were
looking for.

*He turns and leaves into the lift. Joanna is left alone.
She brushes down the bed, straightens the covers. She
sits alone in silence.*

Joanna (*to us*) I don't know why, but I didn't feel anger.
Maybe I was conning myself. Maybe I was too tired to
care. Or maybe I realised what I should have known long
ago. You can't expect too much of a person in a time of
plague.

*She sits on the bed as the door opens and a woman
enters with a case. She doesn't see Joanna. She puts
her case on the bed and starts to unpack her things . . .*

The End.